Edna O'wis

QUICK & EASY RECIPES

Our seal assures you
that every **Better Homes and Gardens**® recipe
in **Quick & Easy Recipes** has been tested
in the Better Homes and Gardens Test Kitchen.
This means that each recipe is practical and reliable,
and meets our high standards of taste appeal.

APPETIZERS & SNACKS

MAIN DISHES

SIDE DISHES

DESSERTS

KRAFT Good Food and Good Food Ideas

KRAFT TIPS

CHEESY BAGELETTE BITES

Combine 2 cups (8 ozs.) 100% Natural KRAFT Shredded Sharp Cheddar Cheese, ½ cup chopped onion, ¼ cup KRAFT Real Mayonnaise and 1 teaspoon Worcestershire sauce; mix well. Split and toast 12 LENDER'S Pretoast Sliced Frozen Plain Bagelettes. Top bagelette halves with cheese mixture. Bake at 350°, 10 minutes. 24 servings.

TROPICAL CHEESE SPREAD

Combine 8-oz. pkg. PHILADELPHIA BRAND Cream Cheese and 8¼ oz. can crushed pineapple, undrained, mixing until well blended. Add 2 cups (8-ozs.) shredded CASINO Brand Natural Monterey Jack Cheese and ½ cup each: flaked coconut, chopped pecans and chopped dried apricots; mix well. Chill. Serve with crackers or French bread slices. 3 cups.

IMPROMPTU APPETIZERS

Pour ¼ cup SAUCEWORKS Cocktail Sauce over 8-oz. pkg. PHILADELPHIA BRAND Cream Cheese; top with ⅓ cup frozen cooked tiny shrimp, thawed. Serve with crackers.

BROILED SWISS RYE APPETIZERS

Combine 1 cup (4 ozs.) 100% Natural KRAFT Shredded Swiss Cheese, cup MIRACLE WHIP Sal Dressing and ¼ cup chopped green pepper; m well. Spread on 18 toaste party rye or pumpernickel bread slices. Broil until lightly browned and chee is melted. 1½ dozen.

As always, 1/2 the calories of butter or margarine

PHILADELPHIA BRAND **CREAM CHEESE** PASTEURIZED KRAFT NET WT. 8 OZS. (227 g)

KRAFT 100% NATURAL SHREDDED LOW-MOISTURE PART-SKIM MOZZARELLA CHEESE Contains 2 CUPS NET WT. 8 OZS. (227g)

CASINO Monterey Jack Natural Cheese NET WT. 8 OZS. (227 g) KRAFT

APPETIZERS & SNACKS

Fiesta Appetizer Pie

Fiesta Appetizer Pie (photo on page 5)

3 **small avocados, peeled, seeded, and cut up**
1 **tablespoon lemon juice**
1 **8-ounce carton dairy sour cream**
1 **8-ounce bottle taco sauce**
2 **green onions, finely chopped**
1 **cup shredded Monterey Jack cheese (4 ounces)**
 Tortilla chips

In a mixing bowl mash the avocados with the lemon juice. Spread mixture evenly in the bottom of a 9-inch pie plate. Spread sour cream evenly over avocado mixture. Spoon taco sauce over sour cream layer. Sprinkle green onions over taco sauce. Top with cheese. Cover and chill for several hours. Serve with chips. Makes about 4 cups.

Pepper and Cheese Squares

½ **cup all-purpose flour**
1 **teaspoon baking powder**
½ **teaspoon salt**
8 **eggs**
3 **cups shredded Monterey Jack cheese (12 ounces)**
1½ **cups cream-style cottage cheese**
3 *or* 4 **pickled jalapeño peppers, rinsed and chopped (about 2 tablespoons)**
2 **tablespoons chopped pimiento**
2 **tablespoons sliced, pitted ripe olives**
 Tortilla chips (optional)

In a bowl stir together flour, baking powder, and salt, then set aside. In large mixer bowl beat eggs with an electric mixer till well combined. Stir flour mixture into beaten eggs and mix well. Fold in Monterey Jack cheese, cottage cheese, peppers, pimiento, and olives.

  Pour into a greased 13x9x2-inch baking dish. Bake in a 350° oven about 40 minutes or till set and golden brown. Let stand 10 minutes. Cut into about 1½-inch squares. Serve warm on tortilla chips, if desired. Makes about 48.

Layered Taco Bean Dip

2 **10½-ounce cans bean dip**
1 **1¼-ounce envelope taco seasoning mix**
6 **green onions, finely chopped**
1 **cup salad dressing *or* mayonnaise**
1 **cup dairy sour cream**
½ **cup sliced, pitted ripe olives**
 Corn chips *or* tortilla chips

In a medium mixing bowl stir together bean dip and taco seasoning mix. Spread mixture on a 10-inch tray or pie plate. Sprinkle with onions. Stir together salad dressing or mayonnaise and sour cream, then spread over onions. Top with olives. Cover and chill for several hours. Serve with chips. Makes 2½ cups.

Fruit-Cheese Dip (on the cover)

1 8-ounce package
   Neufchâtel cheese,
   softened
1 small banana, mashed
¼ teaspoon ground nutmeg
½ cup canned crushed
   pineapple *or* finely
   chopped fresh fruit,
   well drained
   Apple wedges, pear
   wedges, strawberries,
   or other fruit dippers

In a small mixing bowl stir together Neufchâtel cheese, banana, and nutmeg till smooth. Stir in crushed pineapple or chopped fruit. Cover and chill in the refrigerator at least 1 hour. Serve with apple wedges, pear wedges, strawberries, or other fruit dippers as desired. Makes 1¾ cups (14 servings).

Also serve Fruit-Cheese Dip as a dessert. Serve with fruit dippers or cake cubes.

Cheeseball with Everything

2 cups shredded Swiss
   cheese (8 ounces)
2 cups shredded cheddar
   cheese (8 ounces)
1 8-ounce package cream
   cheese, softened
½ cup dairy sour cream
10 slices bacon, crisp-cooked,
   drained, and crumbled
½ cup finely chopped onion
½ cup finely chopped pecans
1 2-ounce jar diced pimiento
2 tablespoons sweet pickle
   relish
   Dash salt
   Dash pepper
¼ cup snipped parsley
1 tablespoon poppy seed
   Assorted crackers

Bring Swiss cheese and cheddar cheese to room temperature. In a large mixer bowl beat together cream cheese and sour cream till fluffy. Beat in Swiss cheese, cheddar cheese, *half* of the bacon, onion, *half* of the pecans, *undrained* pimiento, pickle relish, salt, and pepper till combined. Cover and chill for several hours or till firm.

In a small mixing bowl combine remaining bacon, remaining pecans, parsley, and poppy seed. Shape cheese mixture into a ball, then roll in bacon mixture. Wrap tightly and chill.

Let cheese ball stand at room temperature about 30 minutes before serving. Serve with crackers. Makes 1 large ball.

Cracker Fix-Ups

IDEA 2

Spread *rye crackers* with *soft-style cream cheese.* Top with canned *sardines* and finely chopped *tomato.*

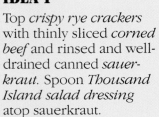

IDEA 1

Top *crispy rye crackers* with thinly sliced *corned beef* and rinsed and well-drained canned *sauerkraut.* Spoon *Thousand Island salad dressing* atop sauerkraut.

IDEA 4

Spread *rye crackers* with *braunschweiger or liverwurst.* Top with slices of *dill pickle* and finely chopped *red onion.*

IDEA 3

Combine equal amounts of *mayonnaise* and grated *Parmesan cheese.* Stir in some snipped *parsley.* Spread on *melba toast rounds.* Broil about 1 minute or till golden.

IDEA 5

Spread *graham crackers* with *peanut butter.* Sprinkle with *miniature semisweet chocolate pieces or coconut.*

IDEA 6

Spread *soft-style cream cheese* on *wheat crackers.* Top with dollops of *orange marmalade* or *red raspberry jelly.*

IDEA 7

Top *graham crackers* with some *pressurized whipped dessert topping* and thin slices of *apple or pear.*

IDEA 8

Spread *water crackers* with *soft-style cream cheese with chives and onion.* Top with thinly sliced *smoked red salmon* and fresh *dill.*

IDEA 9

Top *assorted crackers* with sliced *Monterey Jack cheese with jalapeño peppers.* Top with some *salsa.* If desired, broil for 30 to 60 seconds or till cheese melts.

Beer-Cheese Dip

⅓ cup beer *or* apple juice
Several dashes bottled hot
  pepper sauce
1 cup cubed pasteurized
  process cheese spread
  (4 ounces)
2 tablespoons canned diced
  green chili peppers
  (optional)
1 tablespoon all-purpose
  flour
½ teaspoon dry mustard
1 to 2 tablespoons milk
  (optional)
  Assorted unsalted crackers,
  chips, *or* vegetable
  dippers

In a 1-quart microwave-safe casserole combine beer or apple juice and hot pepper sauce. Micro-cook, uncovered, on 100% power (high) for 1 to 2 minutes or till very hot. Meanwhile, toss together process cheese spread; chili peppers, if desired; flour; and mustard. Stir into beer mixture. Cook, uncovered, on high for 2 to 4 minutes or till process cheese spread melts and mixture is heated through, stirring after every minute. Stir in enough milk to make of dipping consistency. Serve with crackers, chips, or vegetable dippers. Makes ¾ cup dip.

Peppy Artichoke Spread

1 14-ounce can artichoke
  hearts, drained
1 6-ounce jar marinated
  artichoke hearts,
  drained
1 cup shredded cheddar
  cheese (4 ounces)
1 4-ounce can diced green
  chili peppers, drained
  Party rye *or* pumpernickel
  bread

Place drained artichoke hearts in a blender container or food processor bowl. Cover and process until finely chopped, stopping machine to scrape down sides as necessary.

Transfer artichokes to a medium saucepan, then stir in cheese and chili peppers. Cook and stir over medium-low heat for 12 to 15 minutes or till heated through and cheese is melted. Serve warm with rye or pumpernickel bread. Makes about 2½ cups.

Easy Tuna Spread

1 8-ounce package cream
  cheese, cut up
3 tablespoons salsa
1 tablespoon dried parsley
  flakes
1 teaspoon dried minced
  onion
1 6½-ounce can tuna,
  drained and flaked
  Party rye bread *or* assorted
  crackers

In a mixing bowl combine cream cheese, salsa, parsley, and onion; mix till well blended. Fold in tuna. Serve with party rye bread or crackers. Makes 1½ cups spread.

Ham 'n' Cheddar Spread

1　**8-ounce container soft-style cream cheese with chives and onion**
1　**teaspoon prepared mustard**
⅓　**cup finely chopped fully cooked ham**
¼　**cup shredded cheddar cheese (1 ounce)**
　　Crackers, bread *or* celery sticks

In a small mixing bowl stir together cream cheese and mustard.

Stir in ham and cheddar cheese. Cover and chill. Spread on crackers, bread, or celery sticks. Cover and store leftover spread in the refrigerator for up to 5 days. Makes 3 or 4 servings.

Beef 'n' Swiss Spread: Prepare spread as directed above, *except* substitute *cooked roast beef* for the ham and *Swiss cheese* for the cheddar.

Turkey 'n' Mozzarella Spread: Prepare spread as directed above, *except* substitute *cooked turkey* for the ham and *mozzarella cheese* for the cheddar.

Triple Cheese Spread with Crudités

1　**cup low-fat cottage cheese**
½　**cup shredded Swiss cheese (2 ounces)**
¼　**cup grated Parmesan cheese**
2　**tablespoons skim milk**
⅛　**teaspoon dried dillweed**
⅛　**teaspoon pepper**
¼　**cup unsalted sunflower nuts**
¼　**cup finely shredded carrot**
1½　**cups assorted fresh vegetables (cauliflower flowerets, cucumber spears, bias-sliced carrots, *or* green pepper wedges)**

In a blender container or food processor bowl combine cottage cheese, Swiss cheese, Parmesan cheese, milk, dillweed, and pepper. Cover and process till smooth. Transfer to a container. Stir in sunflower nuts and carrot. Cover and chill. Serve with fresh vegetables. Makes 1⅓ cups (4 servings).

Tomato-Avocado Dip

2 slices bacon
1 large avocado, halved, seeded, and peeled
1 medium tomato, peeled, seeded, and finely chopped
½ cup dairy sour cream
¼ cup grated Parmesan cheese
2 green onions, finely chopped
1 tablespoon lemon juice
   Dash bottled hot pepper sauce
1 tablespoon milk (optional)
   Assorted vegetable dippers

In a small skillet cook bacon till crisp. Drain well. Crumble bacon and set aside.

In a medium bowl mash avocado. Stir in tomato, sour cream, Parmesan cheese, green onion, lemon juice, hot pepper sauce, and reserved bacon. Add milk to thin the consistency of the dip, if desired.

Transfer mixture to a serving bowl. Cover and chill. Serve with vegetable dippers. Makes 2 cups.

Pepperoni Cheese Wheel

1 8-ounce container soft-style cream cheese with chives and onion
1¼ cups shredded Muenster cheese (5 ounces)
1 3½-ounce package sliced pepperoni, finely chopped
1 tablespoon milk
2 teaspoons paprika
½ teaspoon ground red pepper
   Assorted crackers *or* melba toast rounds

In a mixing bowl stir together cream cheese, Muenster cheese, chopped pepperoni, and milk. Shape cheese mixture into a 4-inch ball. Flatten the ball into a wheel shape measuring 4½x1½ inches.

On waxed paper combine paprika and red pepper. Roll and pat cheese wheel in paprika mixture till well coated. Cover and refrigerate for 3 hours to 1 week.

Or, wrap the cheese wheel in moisture- and vaporproof material. Seal, label, and freeze for up to 3 months. Before serving, thaw the cheese wheel overnight in the refrigerator.

Use a sharp knife to score the top of the cheese wheel into diamonds. Serve with crackers or melba toast. Makes 14 to 16 servings.

Pepperoni Cheese Wheel

Hot Cheese Dip

¼ **cup finely chopped onion**
1 **tablespoon margarine *or* butter**
1 **teaspoon cornstarch**
¼ **teaspoon pepper**
½ **cup milk**
1 **tablespoon Worcestershire sauce**
2 **cups cubed pasteurized process cheese spread (8 ounces)**
1 **3-ounce package cream cheese, cubed**
1 **tablespoon snipped parsley Assorted unsalted crackers, chips, *or* vegetable dippers, *or* all three**

In a 1½-quart casserole combine onion and margarine or butter. Cook, covered, on 100% power (high) for 1½ to 2½ minutes or till onion is tender, stirring once. Stir in cornstarch and pepper. Add milk and Worcestershire sauce. Cook, uncovered, for 2 to 4½ minutes or till slightly thickened and bubbly, stirring every minute (mixture will appear curdled). Stir in process cheese spread, cream cheese, and parsley. Cook uncovered, on high for 4 to 5 minutes or till cheese is melted and mixture is heated through, stirring every minute.

Keep dip warm in a fondue pot over fondue burner, or reheat in casserole, as necessary, on 50% power (medium) for 2 to 3 minutes. Serve with crackers, chips, or vegetables. Makes 2 cups (8 servings).

Greek-Style Pastries *Fix'n Freeze*

6 **cups torn spinach (8 ounces)**
2 **3-ounce packages cream cheese, softened**
½ **cup crumbled feta cheese (2 ounces)**
¼ **cup grated Parmesan cheese Dash pepper**
15 **sheets frozen phyllo dough (18x14-inch rectangles), thawed**
⅔ **cup margarine *or* butter, melted**

For filling, rinse spinach in cool water. In a large saucepan cook spinach, covered, in just the water that clings to the spinach. Reduce heat when steam forms; cook, covered, about 3 minutes or till tender. Drain well. In a small mixing bowl stir together cream cheese, feta cheese, Parmesan cheese, and pepper. Stir in spinach; set aside.

Unfold phyllo dough; cover with a damp towel or clear plastic wrap. Spread 1 sheet of phyllo dough flat. Brush with some of the melted margarine or butter. Top with another sheet of phyllo dough. Brush with more margarine or butter. Add another sheet, making a total of 3 sheets of phyllo dough; brush with margarine or butter.

Cut the stack, crosswise, into 2-inch strips. Place 1 rounded teaspoon of filling near the end of each strip of phyllo. Starting at the end, fold the dough repeatedly over the filling, forming a triangle that encloses the filling.

Repeat with remaining dough and filling. Brush the tops of each triangle with the remaining margarine or butter. Transfer to a freezer container or bags. Seal, label, and freeze.

To serve, arrange frozen pastries on an ungreased baking sheet. Bake in a 375° oven for 15 to 20 minutes or till puffed and brown. Serve warm or cool. Makes 45 pastries.

Merrymakers' Mushrooms

16 to 20 large fresh mushrooms
1 small zucchini, shredded (¾ cup)
2 tablespoons sliced green onion
⅓ cup grated Parmesan cheese

Remove the stems from the mushrooms. Set the mushroom caps aside. Chop the stems.

In a medium saucepan combine mushroom stems, zucchini, green onion, and 1 tablespoon *water*. Cook and stir over medium heat till vegetables are tender. Drain. Stir Parmesan cheese into vegetable mixture.

Divide vegetable mixture among the mushroom caps. Place stuffed mushrooms in a 13x9x2-inch baking dish. Bake in a 375° oven for 8 to 10 minutes or till mushroom caps are tender. Serve warm. Makes 16 to 20 appetizers.

Spinach Nuggets

2 **10-ounce packages frozen chopped spinach**
1 **tablespoon dried minced onion**
3 **tablespoons margarine *or* butter**
1 **cup herb-seasoned stuffing mix**
1 **cup grated Parmesan cheese**
2 **beaten eggs**

In a saucepan cook the spinach and dried onion according to spinach package directions. Drain well.

In a mixing bowl stir together hot spinach mixture and margarine or butter till butter melts. Add stuffing mix and cheese. Stir in eggs. Shape into 1-inch balls. (If desired, place spinach balls in a shallow pan. Cover and freeze about 1 hour or till firm. Transfer spinach balls to freezer containers. Seal, label, and freeze up to 4 months.)

Place *unfrozen* spinach balls on a greased baking sheet. Bake in a 375° oven about 7 minutes or till heated through. (Or, place *frozen* spinach balls in a shallow baking pan. Bake in a 375° oven for 15 to 20 minutes or till heated through.) Makes about 48.

Microwave: Place frozen spinach and dried onion in a 1-quart nonmetal casserole with 2 tablespoons *water.* Micro-cook, covered, on 100% power (high) for 9 to 11 minutes, stirring once. Let stand 3 minutes. Drain well.

In the same casserole stir together hot spinach mixture and margarine or butter till it melts. Add stuffing mix and Parmesan cheese. Stir in eggs. Shape as above. Freeze, if desired.

Place *half* of the spinach balls in a 12x7½x2-inch nonmetal baking dish. Cook *unfrozen* balls, uncovered, on 100% power (high) for 2 to 3 minutes or till heated through. Repeat with remaining balls. (Or, cook *frozen* spinach balls, uncovered, for 3 to 4 minutes.)

Cheesy Garlic Crisps

¼ **cup margarine *or* butter, melted**
1 **large clove garlic, minced**
24 **slices party rye bread *or* four 6-inch flour tortillas**
¼ **cup grated Parmesan cheese**

In a small mixing bowl combine melted margarine or butter and garlic. (If using tortillas, cut each into 6 wedges.) Brush one side of each rye bread slice or both sides of each tortilla wedge with some of the margarine mixture. Place on a baking sheet in a 350° oven for 5 minutes. Turn over and sprinkle with cheese. Bake for 5 to 7 minutes more or till crisp and golden brown. Makes 24.

Garlic Crisps: Prepare the margarine mixture and bread or tortilla wedges as above, *except* omit sprinkling with the Parmesan cheese.

Parmesan Potato Crisps

3 *or* 4 small baking potatoes
2 teaspoons margarine, melted
¼ cup grated Parmesan cheese
Dash pepper

Scrub potatoes; thinly slice (you should have 2 cups sliced potatoes). Arrange potatoes in a thin layer in a lightly greased 15x10x1-inch baking pan. Brush with melted margarine.

Sprinkle cheese and pepper over potatoes. Bake, uncovered, in a 450° oven for 18 to 20 minutes or till potatoes are brown and crisp. Serves 4.

Fast Cheese Sticks

⅓ cup sandwich spread
¼ cup grated Parmesan cheese
½ teaspoon Italian seasoning
3 hot dog buns, split

Preheat the broiler. In a small bowl stir together sandwich spread, Parmesan cheese, and Italian seasoning.

Spread *1 tablespoon* sandwich spread mixture on cut side of each bun half. Bias-cut each in half lengthwise.

Arrange on a baking sheet. Broil 3 to 4 inches from heat for 2 to 3 minutes or till golden. Makes 3 or 4 servings.

Breadstick Snacks

1 8-ounce container soft-style cream cheese
½ cup shredded cheddar cheese (2 ounces)
2 tablespoons milk
½ teaspoon curry powder *or* chili powder
Breadsticks

In a medium mixing bowl combine cream cheese, cheddar cheese, milk and curry or chili powder. Beat till well mixed.

Dip breadsticks into cheese mixture. Store any remaining cheese mixture, covered, in the refrigerator for up to 3 days. Makes 1¼ cups dip.

Dippity Stix

1 8-ounce package soft-style cream cheese with strawberries *or* pineapple
1 7-ounce jar marshmallow creme
2 tablespoons orange juice
Assorted fruit dippers

In a mixer bowl beat cream cheese, marshmallow creme, and orange juice till smooth. Serve with fruit skewered on wooden toothpicks, like kabobs. Makes 1½ cups dip.

Also serve Dippity Stix as a dessert.

Rice Cake S'mores

Peanut butter (optional)
1 **plain rice cake**
½ **of a 1- to 1½-ounce bar milk chocolate**
12 **tiny marshmallows**

If desired, spread peanut butter on rice cake. On a microwave-safe plate top rice cake with chocolate, then marshmallows. Do not cover. Micro-cook on 100% power (high) for 18 to 20 seconds. Let stand for 30 to 60 seconds. Makes 1 serving.

Minty Rice Cake S'more: Prepare as directed, *except* substitute 2 cream-filled chocolate-covered *peppermint patties* for the milk chocolate.

MAIN DISHES

Taco Casserole

KRAFT *Good Food and Good Food Ideas*

KRAFT TIPS

SPAGHETTI PARMESAN

Heat 32-oz. jar (3½ cups) spaghetti sauce according to label directions. When heated, stir in ⅔ cup KRAFT 100% Grated Parmesan Cheese. Simmer 10 minutes, stirring occasionally. Cook 16-oz. pkg. spaghetti according to package directions. Drain. Pour sauce over spaghetti. Sprinkle with additional parmesan cheese. 6 to 8 servings.

POTLUCK SUPPER

Prepare 14-oz. pkg. KRAFT Deluxe Macaroni and Cheese Dinner as directed on package. Add 2 cups chopped cooked chicken and ½ cup sour cream; mix well. Heat thoroughly, stirring occasionally. 5 servings.

FRUIT 'N CHEESY GRILL

Combine ½ cup each, chopped pitted dates, chopped walnuts, raisins and ⅓ cup KRAFT Real Mayonnaise; mix lightly. Cover each of 4 whole-wheat bread slices with one VELVEETA Pasteurized Process Cheese Spread Slice, ⅓ cup fruit mixtu a second process cheese spread slice and a second bread slice. Spread sandwich with PARKAY Margarine. G until lightly browned o both sides. 4 sandwic

KRAFT Sandwich Spread
16 FL. OZS. (1 PT.) (0.47 L)

KRAFT 100% Grated Parmesan Cheese *Italian type*
The Secret to Thicker Sauce
NET WT. 8 OZS. (227g)

SAVORY CHEESY TORTELLINI

Cube ½ lb. VELVEETA Pasteurized Process Cheese Spread. Combine with ¼ cup milk and ½ teaspoon ground nutmeg in saucepan. Stir over low heat until process cheese spread is melted. Toss with 7-oz. pkg. cheese filled tortellini, cooked, drained. 4 servings.

CRUSTLESS GREEK QUICHE

Cook and drain 10-oz. pkg. frozen chopped spinach. Combine with 4 beaten eggs, 4-ozs. (¾ cup) crumbled CHURNY Feta Cheese, ½ cup milk and ¼ cup chopped onion; mix well. Bake at 325°, 35 minutes or until set. Garnish with black olives. 6 servings.

CHICKEN FUN-WICH

Combine 5-oz. can chunk chicken, ¼ cup KRAFT Sandwich Spread and 2 tablespoons chopped green pepper; mix lightly. Spread four whole-wheat bread slices with sandwich spread. Top each slice with lettuce, sliced tomato and chicken mixture. Top with second bread slice spread with sandwich spread. 4 sandwiches.

KRAFT TIPS

ONE PAN SWEET AND SOUR CHICKEN

1 14-oz. pkg. KRAFT Sweet and Sour
Applause Oven Bake Dinner
5 chicken breast halves, skinned
1 8¼-oz. can pineapple chunks
1 6-oz. pkg. frozen pea pods,
   thawed, drained

Combine Rice, Seasoning Mix and
1¾ cups cold water in 13 x 9-inch
baking dish or pan; stir until
blended. Top with chicken breasts.
Cover tightly with foil. Bake at 375°,
50 minutes. Remove foil. Drain pineapple, reserving liquid. Arrange
pineapple and pea pods around
chicken pieces. Cut off corner of
Sweet and Sour Sauce pouch with
scissors; combine with 3 tablespoons reserved pineapple liquid.
Distribute evenly over chicken, pineapple and pea pods. Continue baking, uncovered, 10 minutes. Let
stand 5 minutes.

5 servings

Prep time: 10 minutes
Cooking time: 60 minutes plus standing

QUICK SOUTHERN STYLE CHILI

1 lb. ground beef
1 lb. ground pork
1 cup chopped onion
1 garlic clove, minced
1 28-oz. can tomatoes, undrained, cut
   up
2 cups water
1 6-oz. can tomato paste
1 16-oz. can kidney beans, drained
1 16-oz. can green chilies, drained
1 4-oz. CARROLL SHELBY'S ORIGINAL
   TEXAS BRAND Chili Mix
1 pkg. 100% Natural KRAFT Shredded Cheddar
   Cheese
Chopped green pepper
Chopped onion

Brown meat in large saucepan; drain.
Add onions and garlic; cook until tender.
Add tomatoes, 1½ cups water and
tomato paste. Stir in kidney beans and
chillies. Add Large Spice packet, Salt and
Cayenne Pepper to taste. Cover; simmer
15 minutes, stirring occasionally. Gradually add ½ cup water to Masa Flour,
stirring until well blended. Add to meat
mixture, continue simmering 5 minutes.
Top with cheese, green pepper and onion.

Nine 1-cup servings

Prep time: 10 minutes
Cooking time: 25 minutes
Variation: Omit ground pork. Increase
ground beef to 2 pounds.

EASY TEX-MEX BARBECUE

1 14-oz. pkg. KRAFT Barbecue
Chicken Applause Oven Bake Dinner
⅓ cup onion slices
1 4-oz. can chopped green chilies,
   drained
5 chicken breast halves, skinned

Combine Potatoes, Seasoning Mix
and 2½ cups cold water in 13 x 9-
inch baking dish or pan; stir until
blended. Top with onions, chilies
and chicken breasts. Cover tightly
with foil. Bake at 375°, 55 minutes.
Remove foil. Cut off corner of Barbecue Sauce pouch with scissors; distribute evenly over chicken. Continue
baking, uncovered, 10 minutes. Let
stand 5 minutes.

5 servings

Prep time: 10 minutes
Cooking time: 65 minutes plus standing

CHILI PIE

2 lbs. ground beef
2 cups cold water
1 8-oz. can tomato sauce
1 pkg. CARROLL SHELBY'S ORIGI
   TEXAS BRAND Chili Mix
1 15-oz. pkg. corn bread mix
1 8-oz. pkg. 100% Natural KRAFT
   Shredded Sharp Cheddar Cheese

Brown meat in large saucepan; dr
Add water and tomato sauce. Brin
boil; reduce heat. Simmer 15 min
stirring occasionally. Stir in Large
Packet. Gradually add ½ cup wat
Masa Flour, stirring until well ble
Add to meat mixture, mix well. Co
simmering 15 minutes, stirring
occasionally.

Prepare corn bread mix as direct
package. Spread into greased 15
1-inch jelly roll pan. Spoon Chili
corn bread mixture. Bake at 350°
25 minutes or until golden brown
kle with cheese; continue baking
utes or until cheese is melted. C
squares.

12 servings

Prep time: 10 minutes
Cooking time: 30 minutes
Baking time: 30 minutes
Make Ahead: Prepare Chili as dir
Cover, refrigerate. When ready t
continue as directed.

22

Pizza Pork Chops

4 **pork chops, cut ¾ inch**
   thick
1 **small onion, chopped**
3 **tablespoons margarine** *or*
   butter
1 **8-ounce package (2 cups)**
   herb-seasoned stuffing
   mix
½ **cup water**
¼ **teaspoon dried oregano,**
   crushed
1 **8-ounce can pizza sauce**
1 **3-ounce can sliced**
   mushrooms, drained
1 **4-ounce package shredded**
   mozzarella cheese

Trim excess fat from chops; set chops aside. In medium saucepan cook onion in margarine or butter till tender but not brown. Add stuffing mix, water, and oregano to cooked onion; stir till well combined.

In a 12x7½x2-inch baking dish divide stuffing mixture into 4 mounds (put about ½ cup stuffing in each mound and shape with your hands). Place a pork chop atop each stuffing mound. Pour the pizza sauce over the pork chops. Sprinkle the drained mushrooms atop the sauce. Cover with foil and bake in 350° oven about 1 hour or till chops are tender. Sprinkle chops with shredded cheese. Makes 4 servings.

Blue Cheese Burgers

1 **beaten egg**
1 **tablespoon Worcestershire**
   sauce
⅓ **cup fine dry rye bread**
   crumbs
1 **teaspoon prepared**
   mustard
⅛ **teaspoon pepper**
   Dash garlic powder
1½ **pounds lean ground beef**
¾ **cup crumbled blue cheese**
6 **hamburger buns, split and**
   toasted
   Alfalfa sprouts

In a medium mixing bowl combine egg and Worcestershire sauce. Stir in rye bread crumbs, mustard, pepper, and garlic powder. Add ground beef and mix well. Shape the meat mixture into twelve ¼-inch-thick patties.

Place about *2 tablespoons* blue cheese atop each of *6 patties*. Spread to within ½ inch of edges. Top with remaining patties. Press meat around edges to seal well.

Place patties on a rack in an unheated broiler pan. Broil 3 to 4 inches from the heat about 13 minutes total or till done, turning once. *Or,* grill patties, on an uncovered grill, directly over *medium-hot* coals for 13 to 14 minutes total or till done, turning once. Serve burgers on buns with alfalfa sprouts. Serves 6.

Cheesy Italian Pie

1 **15-ounce package (2**
   crusts) folded refrigerated
   unbaked pie crusts
1 **10-ounce package frozen**
   chopped spinach
1 **pound ground beef**
2 **8-ounce cans pizza sauce**
2 **beaten eggs**
1 **cup ricotta cheese** *or*
   cottage cheese
½ **cup grated Parmesan**
   cheese
⅛ **teaspoon dried marjoram,**
   crushed
   All-purpose flour

Let pie crusts stand at room temperature while preparing filling. In a colander run hot water over spinach about 5 minutes or till partially thawed. Drain well, squeezing out excess liquid.

Meanwhile, in a large skillet cook ground beef till brown. Drain off fat. Stir in pizza sauce and spinach.

In a bowl stir together eggs, ricotta or cottage cheese, Parmesan cheese, and marjoram. Sprinkle flour on pie crusts according to package directions. Line a 9-inch pie plate with *one* pie crust. Spoon ricotta mixture into crust. Top with beef mixture. Place remaining crust over filling. Seal and flute edges. Cut slits in top crust to allow steam to escape. Bake in a 425° oven about 25 minutes or till crust is golden. Makes 6 servings.

Greek Feta Casserole

2 **cups hot water**
3 **ounces elbow macaroni (¾ cup)**
1 **slightly beaten egg**
½ **cup crumbled feta cheese (2 ounces)**
¼ **cup milk**
¾ **pound ground lamb *or* ground pork**
1 **teaspoon dried minced onion**
1 **8-ounce can tomato sauce**
½ **teaspoon ground cinnamon**
½ **cup crumbled feta cheese (2 ounces)**

In a 3-quart saucepan bring water to boiling. Add macaroni. Reduce heat slightly. Cook in gently boiling water about 10 minutes or till tender. Drain well.

In a mixing bowl combine egg, ½ cup feta cheese, and milk. Add drained pasta, tossing gently. Spread pasta mixture evenly in an 8x8x2-inch baking dish.

In a large skillet cook ground lamb or pork and onion till meat is brown. Drain off fat. Stir in the tomato sauce and ground cinnamon and heat through.

Spread meat mixture over pasta mixture in baking dish. Sprinkle with ½ cup cheese. Bake in a 375° oven for 8 to 10 minutes or till heated through. Makes 4 servings.

Pizza Casserole

6 **ounces fettucine, broken**
1 **3½-ounce package sliced pepperoni**
1 **15½-ounce jar pizza sauce**
½ **of a 12-ounce package (1½ cups) shredded mozzarella cheese**
1 **4-ounce can sliced mushrooms, drained**
1 **2.25-ounce can sliced pitted ripe olives, drained**
1 **tablespoon grated Parmesan cheese**

Bring 8 cups *hot water* to boiling. Add pasta. Reduce heat. Cook in gently boiling water for 8 to 10 minutes or till tender. Drain. Return to pan. Halve pepperoni; add to pasta. Stir in pizza sauce, *¾ cup* of the mozzarella cheese, mushrooms, olives, and Parmesan. Transfer to a 12x7½x2-inch baking dish. Top with remaining mozzarella cheese. Bake in a 400° oven about 15 minutes or till hot. Serves 6.

Taco Casserole

1 pound ground beef
1 medium onion, chopped
   (½ cup)
1 8-ounce can tomato sauce
¼ cup water
1 teaspoon chili powder
1 16-ounce can refried beans
¼ cup taco sauce
1½ cups shredded Monterey
   Jack cheese (6 ounces)
5 taco or tostado shells,
   coarsely crushed
1 cup shredded lettuce
1 small tomato, chopped
   (¼ cup) (optional)
¼ cup sliced green onion
   (optional)
¼ cup sliced pitted ripe olives
   (optional)
1 6-ounce container frozen
   avocado dip (optional)

Crumble the beef into a 1½-quart casserole, then stir in onion. Micro-cook, covered, on 100% power (HIGH) 4½ to 5½ minutes or till done. Drain, then stir in tomato sauce, water, and chili powder. Micro-cook, covered, on 100% power (HIGH) about 6 minutes or till bubbly.

Meanwhile, stir together beans and taco sauce. Spread in bottom of a 12x7½x2-inch baking dish, then spread the meat mixture atop. Micro-cook, uncovered, on 100% power (HIGH) 7 to 9 minutes or till heated through.

Top with cheese. Micro-cook, uncovered, on 100% power (HIGH) about 1 minute or till cheese is melted.

Top with crushed taco or tostado shells and lettuce. If desired, top with tomato, green onion, olives, and avocado dip. Makes 6 servings.

Taco Burgers

⅓ cup salsa *or* taco sauce
¼ cup fine dry bread crumbs
1 teaspoon chili powder
¼ teaspoon salt
1 pound ground beef
4 lettuce leaves (optional)
4 hamburger buns, split
4 slices pasteurized process
   cheese spread (4 ounces)
   Salsa *or* taco sauce
   (optional)

In a mixing bowl combine salsa or taco sauce, bread crumbs, chili powder, and salt. Add ground beef; mix well. Shape meat mixture into four ¾-inch-thick patties.

Arrange patties in an 8x8x2-inch microwave-safe baking dish. Cover loosely with waxed paper. Micro-cook on 100% power (high) for 3 minutes. Drain off fat, give the dish a half-turn, and turn meat patties over. Cook on high for 3 to 5 minutes more or till no pink remains.

Place lettuce on buns, if desired. Top with cooked meat patties and process cheese spread. Pass additional salsa or taco sauce with burgers, if desired. Makes 4 servings.

Mexican Corn Bread Casserole

¼ cup water
3 tablespoons margarine *or* butter
2¼ cups corn bread stuffing mix, crushed
1 slightly beaten egg
¾ pound ground beef
½ of a medium onion, chopped (¼ cup)
1 8-ounce can red kidney beans, drained
1 cup shredded Monterey Jack cheese with jalapeño peppers (4 ounces)
½ of an 8-ounce can (½ cup) tomato sauce
2 teaspoons chili powder
½ cup shredded Monterey Jack cheese with jalapeño peppers (2 ounces)

In a medium bowl micro-cook water and margarine or butter, uncovered, on 100% power (high) 45 to 60 seconds or till margarine is melted.

Stir in stuffing mix and egg till moistened. Turn crumb mixture into a 9-inch pie plate. Using your hands, press crumb mixture firmly against bottom and sides of pie plate, then set aside.

Crumble beef into the mixing bowl, then stir in onion. Micro-cook, covered, on 100% power (high) about 4 minutes or till beef is done and onion is tender, stirring once to break up beef. Drain off fat.

Stir in kidney beans, cheese, tomato sauce, and chili powder. Turn meat mixture into crust.

Micro-cook, uncovered, on 100% power (high) 6 to 8 minutes or till heated through, rotating the dish every 3 minutes. Top with cheese. Cover and let stand 5 minutes. Makes 6 servings.

Attention Microwave Owners

Recipes with microwave directions in this book were tested in countertop microwave ovens rated at 600 to 700 watts.

Times are approximate because microwave ovens vary by manufacturer.

The best rule of thumb for micro-cooking is to check the food at the end of the *minimum* cooking time given in the recipe. Then add more time as needed to achieve the desired doneness.

Nachos for Dinner!

¾ pound ground beef
⅓ cup taco sauce
4 cups tortilla chips
2 cups shredded Monterey Jack cheese (8 ounces)
Dairy sour cream (optional)
Chopped tomatoes (optional)
Sliced ripe olives (optional)

In a 1½-quart microwave-safe casserole crumble ground beef. Micro-cook, covered, on 100% power (high) for 4 to 6 minutes or till meat is brown, stirring once. Drain fat. Stir in taco sauce.

On each of 2 microwave-safe dinner plates layer *half* of the tortilla chips, meat mixture, and cheese. Cook each plate on high for 1½ to 2½ minutes or till cheese melts. Cook the second plate of nachos while you serve the first.

Serve with sour cream, tomatoes, and olives, if desired. Serves 4.

Conventional Directions: Preheat the broiler. In a small skillet brown ground beef. Drain fat and stir in taco sauce.

On a pizza pan layer all of the chips, meat mixture, and cheese. Broil 4 to 5 inches from the heat for 2 to 3 minutes or till cheese melts. Serve as directed.

Nachos for Dinner

Chili-Frank Burritos

4 **7-inch flour tortillas**
4 **slices pasteurized process cheese spread**
4 **chili-stuffed frankfurters**

Wrap tortillas in foil. Heat in a 375° oven 5 minutes.

On top of each tortilla arrange *one* slice process cheese spread and *one* frankfurter. Fold in ends of tortillas. Roll up tortillas around process cheese spread and frankfurters. Wrap in foil. Bake in the 375° oven about 15 minutes or till warm. Makes 4 servings.

Snowcapped Broccoli 'N' Ham

1 **10-ounce package frozen cut broccoli**
10 **ounces fully cooked ham, chopped (about 2 cups)**
¼ **cup chopped onion**
¾ **cup salad dressing *or* mayonnaise**
3 **egg whites**
1 **teaspoon dry mustard**
2 **tablespoons grated Parmesan cheese**

Place frozen broccoli in a colander. Run hot water over broccoli just till thawed. Drain well. Divide broccoli among four 10-ounce custard cups.

Combine chopped ham, onion, and ¼ *cup* of the salad dressing or mayonnaise. Spoon ham mixture over broccoli in custard cups.

For egg topping, in a small mixer bowl beat egg whites till stiff peaks form (tips stand straight). Stir together the remaining salad dressing and dry mustard. Fold salad dressing mixture into beaten egg whites. Spoon egg mixture over ham mixture in custard cups. Sprinkle with Parmesan cheese.

Bake in a 350° oven for 15 to 18 minutes or till topping is golden. Makes 4 servings.

Chicken Parmesan

3 whole medium chicken breasts (about 2¼ pounds total)
⅓ cup grated Parmesan cheese
¼ teaspoon Italian seasoning, crushed
¼ cup sliced green onion
1 tablespoon margarine *or* butter
1 tablespoon all-purpose flour
½ cup skim milk
½ of a 10-ounce package frozen chopped spinach, thawed and drained
1 tablespoon chopped pimiento

Place one chicken breast on a cutting board, skin side up. Pull the skin away from the meat, then discard skin. Bone chicken breast. Repeat with remaining breasts.

In a small mixing bowl combine Parmesan cheese and Italian seasoning. Roll chicken pieces in cheese mixture to coat lightly; set remaining cheese mixture aside.

Arrange pieces in an 8x8x2-inch baking dish. In a small saucepan cook onion in hot margarine or butter till tender but not brown. Stir in flour, then add milk all at once. Cook and stir till thickened and bubbly; stir in drained spinach and pimiento. Spoon spinach mixture over chicken and sprinkle with remaining cheese mixture. Bake, uncovered, in a 350° oven for 30 to 35 minutes or till tender. Makes 6 servings.

Chicken Divan-Style

1 10-ounce package frozen broccoli *or* asparagus spears
2 tablespoons margarine *or* butter
3 tablespoons all-purpose flour
⅛ teaspoon ground nutmeg
1 cup milk
2 teaspoons lemon juice
½ cup grated Parmesan cheese
10 ounces sliced cooked chicken *or* turkey
4 slices Swiss cheese (4 ounces)
Paprika

Prepare broccoli or asparagus spears according to the package directions. Drain. Arrange in a 10x6x2-inch baking dish. Set aside.

For sauce, in a medium saucepan melt margarine or butter. Stir in flour and nutmeg. Add milk. Cook and stir till thicken and bubbly. Stir in lemon juice.

Pour *half* of the sauce over broccoli or asparagus; sprinkle with *half* of the Parmesan cheese. Top with chicken or turkey and Swiss cheese. Pour remaining sauce over all; sprinkle with remaining Parmesan cheese and paprika. Bake in a 350° oven about 20 minutes or till heated through. Makes 6 servings.

Microwave: In a 10x6x2-inch baking dish combine broccoli or asparagus spears and 2 tablespoons *water.* Micro-cook, covered, on 100% (high) 5 to 7 minutes; give the dish a half-turn once during cooking. Let stand, covered, 3 minutes. Drain.

For sauce, in a 2-cup glass measuring cup cook margarine or butter, uncovered, 30 to 40 seconds or till melted. Stir in flour and nutmeg. Add milk. Cook, uncovered, 3 to 4 minutes or till thickened and bubbly. Stir after each minute. Stir in lemon juice. Pour *half* of the sauce over broccoli or asparagus; sprinkle with *half* of the Parmesan cheese. Top with chicken or turkey and cheese. Pour remaining sauce over all; sprinkle with remaining Parmesan cheese and paprika. Cook, covered with waxed paper, 6 to 7 minutes or till heated through; give dish a half-turn once during cooking. Let stand 5 minutes.

Herbed Chicken À la Française

2 whole medium chicken breasts (about 1½ pounds total), skinned, halved lengthwise, and boned
2 green onions, sliced
½ teaspoon dried tarragon, crushed
1 tablespoon margarine *or* butter
⅓ cup dry white wine *or* chicken broth
1 egg white
½ cup salad dressing *or* mayonnaise
1 tablespoon grated Parmesan cheese
1 tablespoon snipped parsley

Arrange chicken breast halves in a 12x7½x2-inch baking dish. Sprinkle green onion and tarragon atop chicken. Dot with margarine or butter. Season with salt and pepper. Add wine to baking dish.

Bake, uncovered, in a 350° oven for 30 minutes. Remove from oven. In a mixer bowl beat egg white till stiff peaks form. Fold salad dressing or mayonnaise into stiffly beaten egg white. Spoon egg white mixture over chicken breasts. Sprinkle with Parmesan cheese.

Return to oven and bake, uncovered, for 12 to 15 minutes more or till lightly browned. Sprinkle chicken breasts with parsley. Serves 4.

Cheesy Chicken Enchiladas

1 12-ounce jar chunky salsa
2 cups cubed pasteurized process cheese spread (8 ounces)
3 cups chopped, cooked chicken *or* turkey
4 8-inch flour tortillas
1 2¼-ounce can sliced pitted ripe olives, drained and coarsely chopped

For filling, in a medium saucepan combine salsa and process cheese spread. Cook, stirring occasionally, over medium heat till process cheese spread melts; set aside *1¼ cups* sauce. Stir chicken or turkey into remaining sauce. Spoon some of the chicken mixture down center of each tortilla. Roll up tortillas. Place the filled tortillas, seam side down, in a greased 8x8x2-inch baking dish. Cover with foil. Bake in a 375° oven for 15 to 20 minutes or till heated through. To serve, reheat reserved sauce and pour over enchiladas. Sprinkle with olives. Makes 4 servings.

Turkey-Mac Casserole

1 14-ounce package macaroni and cheese dinner mix
1 10-ounce package frozen mixed vegetables
1 pound bulk turkey sausage
½ of a small onion, chopped
¾ cup milk
¼ cup margarine *or* butter
1 3-ounce package cream cheese, cut up

Cook macaroni from mix in a large amount of boiling salted water for 5 minutes. Add frozen vegetables. Cook for 5 minutes more. Drain macaroni-vegetable mixture. Return to saucepan.

Meanwhile, in a medium skillet cook turkey sausage and chopped onion till sausage is well done and onion is tender. Drain, if necessary.

Add cheese sauce from mix, milk, margarine or butter, and cream cheese to the hot macaroni mixture. Stir till margarine or butter and cream cheese are melted. Stir in turkey mixture and heat through. Makes 4 servings.

Chicken with Biscuits

1 **19-ounce can chunky chicken vegetable soup**
1 **cup chopped cooked chicken *or* one 5-ounce can chunk-style chicken**
1 **cup shredded Monterey Jack cheese (4 ounces)**
  Biscuits

In a medium saucepan combine soup, chicken, and cheese. Cook over medium heat till cheese melts and mixture is hot, stirring occasionally.

To serve, spoon chicken mixture into 3 individual bowls. Top with biscuits. Makes 3 servings.

Microwave: In a 1½-quart nonmetal casserole combine soup, chicken, and cheese. Cover and micro-cook on 100% power (high) for 4 to 6 minutes or till mixture is hot and bubbly, stirring once. Serve as directed above.

Easy Cheesy Fish Bake

1 **pound fresh *or* frozen skinless orange roughy, catfish, pike, cod, *or* haddock fish fillets (½ to ¾ inch thick)**
1 **8-ounce jar pasteurized process cheese spread**
¼ **cup milk**
1 **10-ounce package frozen peas**
1 **cup quick-cooking rice**
⅛ **teaspoon dried dillweed**

Thaw fish, if frozen. Cut fillets into 1-inch pieces.

In a 1½-quart casserole stir together process cheese spread and milk. Stir in peas, rice, dillweed, and fish. Bake, covered, in a 375° oven for 40 to 45 minutes or till heated through, stirring once or twice. Makes 4 servings.

Zippy Chicken Casserole

2 cups whole wheat *or* plain elbow macaroni
1 10-ounce package frozen chopped broccoli
¼ cup margarine *or* butter
1 large onion, chopped
½ cup thinly sliced celery
¼ cup all-purpose flour
  Several dashes bottled hot pepper sauce
  Dash pepper
2 cups milk
1½ cups cubed pasteurized process cheese spread (6 ounces)
3 cups chopped cooked chicken *or* turkey
½ cup sliced pitted ripe olives
2 medium tomatoes, sliced
1 6-ounce container frozen Mexican-style avocado dip, thawed
½ cup alfalfa sprouts (optional)

Cook macaroni according to package directions. Drain. Meanwhile, run water over broccoli to thaw.

For sauce, in a large saucepan melt margarine or butter. Add onion and celery. Cook till tender. Stir in flour, pepper sauce, and pepper. Add milk all at once. Cook and stir over medium heat till mixture is thickened and bubbly. Add process cheese spread. Cook and stir till process cheese spread melts.

Add chicken or turkey, olives, macaroni, and broccoli to sauce. Mix well. Turn mixture into a 13x9x2-inch baking dish. Bake, covered, in a 350° oven for 30 minutes. Arrange tomato slices over top. Bake, covered, about 5 minutes more or till heated through.

Spoon avocado dip over top. Sprinkle with alfalfa sprouts, if desired. Serves 8.

Cheesy Chicken Macaroni Casserole

½ cup elbow macaroni
1 10-ounce package frozen peas and carrots
2 tablespoons margarine *or* butter
2 tablespoons all-purpose flour
½ teaspoon dried basil, crushed
1⅓ cups milk
1½ cups cubed pasteurized process cheese spread (6 ounces)
1½ cups chopped cooked chicken *or* turkey, *or* frozen diced cooked chicken, thawed
¾ cup soft bread crumbs (1 slice)
¼ cup chopped almonds
1 tablespoon margarine *or* butter, melted

Cook macaroni according to the package directions. Drain.

Meanwhile, place frozen peas and carrots in a colander. Rinse with running water to separate. Set aside.

In a large saucepan melt 2 tablespoons margarine or butter. Stir in flour and basil. Add milk. Cook and stir till thickened and bubbly. Remove from heat.

Stir in process cheese spread till melted. Stir in macaroni, peas and carrots, and chicken or turkey. Turn mixture into a 1½ quart casserole.

Combine bread crumbs, almonds, and 1 tablespoon melted margarine or butter, then sprinkle over the casserole. Bake, uncovered, in a 350° oven 35 to 40 minutes or till heated through. Serves 6.

Pike with Parmesan

1 **pound fresh *or* frozen northern pike *or* other fish fillets**
1 **beaten egg**
2 **tablespoons milk**
¼ **cup grated Parmesan cheese**
¼ **cup finely crushed wheat wafers**
½ **teaspoon dried basil, crushed**
½ **teaspoon paprika**
⅛ **teaspoon pepper**
2 **tablespoons cooking oil**

Thaw fish, if frozen. Separate fillets or cut into 4 serving-size portions. Rinse and pat dry with paper towels. Measure thickness of fish.

In a shallow dish combine egg and milk. In another shallow dish combine Parmesan cheese, crushed wafers, basil, paprika, and pepper. Dip fish fillets into egg mixture. Then roll fish in crumb mixture. Place coated fish in a greased shallow baking pan.

Drizzle cooking oil over fish. Bake in a 500° oven till golden and fish flakes easily with a fork. Allow 4 to 6 minutes for each ½ inch of thickness. Makes 4 servings.

Flounder and Spinach Bake

1 **pound fresh *or* frozen flounder *or* sole fillets**
1 **10-ounce package frozen chopped spinach, thawed and well drained**
1½ **cups seasoned croutons, coarsely crushed**
1 **8-ounce can whole kernel corn, drained**
¾ **cup shredded Swiss cheese (3 ounces)**
1 **beaten egg**
3 **tablespoons water**
  Salt
  Lemon pepper *or* pepper
1 **medium tomato, cut into 12 thin wedges**
¼ **cup shredded Swiss cheese (1 ounce)**

Thaw fish fillets, if frozen. Combine spinach, croutons, corn, and cheese. Combine egg and water. Add to spinach mixture; mix well.

Spread spinach mixture evenly in a 12x7½x2-inch baking dish. Cover with foil. Bake in a 375° oven for 10 minutes. Arrange fish fillets over spinach mixture, overlapping if necessary. Sprinkle with salt and lemon pepper or pepper.

Cover with foil. Bake for 15 minutes. Remove foil. Arrange tomato wedges on fillets. Sprinkle with cheese. Bake about 5 minutes more or till fish flakes easily with a fork. Makes 6 servings.

Microwave: Thaw fish fillets, if frozen. Prepare spinach mixture as directed above. Spread mixture in a 12x7½x2-inch microwave-safe baking dish. Cover with vented microwave-safe plastic wrap. Micro-cook on 100% power (high) for 3 minutes. Arrange fish fillets over spinach mixture. Cook, covered, on high for 3 minutes. Arrange tomato wedges on fillets. Sprinkle with ¼ cup cheese. Cook, covered, on high for 1½ to 2½ minutes or till fish flakes easily with a fork.

Quick tip

Testing Fish for Doneness

Sometimes it's hard to tell when fish is done. The best way to test for doneness is to poke a fork into the thickest portion of the fish at a 45-degree angle and twist gently. If the fish flakes easily and looks opaque, as shown, it's done. If the fish resists flaking and still looks translucent, continue cooking it. Fish cooks quickly, so test it frequently.

Mexican-Style Fish Sticks

16 **frozen fish sticks**
 1 **8½ ounce package corn muffin mix**
 1 **4-ounce can diced green chili peppers, drained**
 1 **cup cubed pasteurized process cheese spread, (4 ounces)**
  Taco sauce (optional)

Arrange fish sticks in a greased 9x9x2-inch baking pan. Bake in a 400° oven for 25 minutes. Meanwhile, prepare muffin mix according to package directions; stir in chili peppers and process cheese spread. Spread evenly over fish sticks in the baking pan. Return to the oven and bake about 25 minutes more or till corn bread is done. To serve, cut into squares or rectangles; carefully remove from the pan. Serve warm with taco sauce, if desired. Makes 6 servings.

Scrambled Egg Casserole

¼ **cup chopped green pepper**
 2 **tablespoons margarine *or* butter**
 6 **beaten eggs**
 1 **8-ounce jar pasteurized process cheese spread**
 2 **tablespoons milk**
 2 **tablespoons chopped pimiento**
  Dash pepper
¾ **cup soft bread crumbs**
 1 **tablespoon margarine *or* butter, melted**

In skillet cook green pepper in the 2 tablespoons margarine or butter till tender. Add eggs and scramble just till set. Turn into a 1-quart casserole; set aside. In a small bowl stir together process cheese spread and milk. Stir in pimiento and pepper. Pour mixture over the scrambled eggs in casserole. Combine the bread crumbs and the 1 tablespoon melted margarine or butter. Bake, uncovered, in 350° oven for about 20 minutes or till heated through. (*Or;* cover and chill overnight. Bake, uncovered, in 350° oven for 25 to 30 minutes or till heated through.) Makes 4 servings.

Skillet Potato Breakfast

6 **slices bacon**
 3 **cups frozen hash brown potatoes with onions and peppers**
 1 **cup shredded Monterey Jack cheese (4 ounces)**
 4 **eggs**

In a 10-inch skillet cook bacon till crisp. Drain; reserve 2 tablespoons drippings in skillet. Set bacon aside.

Cook frozen hash brown potatoes in reserved drippings till golden. Crumble 2 slices of the bacon; stir into potatoes. Sprinkle shredded cheese atop potatoes. Place remaining 4 slices of bacon in an X atop cheese.

Carefully break 1 egg into each triangle formed by bacon. Cover; cook over medium heat about 6 minutes or till eggs are set. Makes 4 servings.

Macaroni and Cheese

1½ cups elbow macaroni
  (6 ounces)
¼ cup finely chopped onion
3 tablespoons margarine *or*
  butter
2 tablespoons all-purpose
  flour
¼ teaspoon salt
2½ cups milk
2 cups cubed pasteurized
  process cheese spread
  (8 ounces)
1 medium tomato, sliced

Cook macaroni according to package directions. Drain.

For cheese sauce, in a large saucepan cook onion in margarine or butter till tender but not brown. Stir in the flour, salt, and dash *pepper*. Add milk all at once. Cook and stir till thickened and bubbly. Add process cheese spread; stir till melted.

Stir macaroni into sauce. Turn into a 1½-quart casserole. Bake in a 350° oven for 20 minutes. Arrange tomato slices on top. Bake for 5 to 10 minutes more or till heated through. Makes 4 main-dish servings or 8 side-dish servings.

Mac and Cheese Special

1 14-ounce package
  macaroni and cheese
  dinner mix
½ cup sour cream and
  buttermilk dip, sour
  cream dip with toasted
  onion, *or* sour cream dip
  with chives
8 ounces frankfurters
  (4 or 5), cut lengthwise
  and sliced ½ inch thick

Prepare mix according to package directions.

Stir in dip, then frankfurters. Heat through. Makes 4 to 6 servings.

Twisty Macaroni and Cheese

1½ cups corkscrew *or* elbow
  macaroni
2 slices bacon
1 cup frozen broccoli cuts
2 tablespoons water
1 8-ounce jar pasteurized
  process cheese spread

Cook macaroni according to package directions; drain and set aside. Meanwhile, place bacon in a 1½-quart microwave-safe casserole. Cover and cook in a microwave oven on 100% (high) power for 1 to 2 minutes or till crisp; drain and crumble. Use a paper towel to wipe out the casserole. In same casserole combine broccoli and water. Micro-cook on high for 3 to 5 minutes or till crisp-tender; drain. Stir in process cheese spread. Micro-cook, uncovered, on high for 1 minute. Stir in cooked macaroni. Micro-cook on high for 2 to 3 minutes or till heated through, stirring once. Sprinkle with bacon. Makes 4 servings.

Mac 'n' Cheese Fix-Ups

IDEA 1

Stir together 2 cups creamy deli *coleslaw* and 1 prepared 14-ounce package *deluxe type macaroni-and-cheese mix*. Chill in the refrigerator for 3 to 24 hours, if desired. Stir in ¼ cup *milk* to moisten, if necessary.

IDEA 2

Stir together 1 prepared 14-ounce package *deluxe type macaroni-and-cheese mix*, ½ cup *buttermilk salad dressing*, and ¼ teaspoon *pepper*. Fold in 1 cup frozen *peas*. Chill in the refrigerator for 3 to 24 hours, if desired. Stir in ¼ cup *milk* to moisten, if necessary.

IDEA 3

Stir together one 8½-ounce can *peas and carrots*, drained; 1 prepared 14-ounce package *deluxe type macaroni-and-cheese mix;* and one 6½-ounce can *tuna*, drained and flaked. Heat through.

IDEA 4

Stir together 8 ounces fully cooked smoked *turkey sausage,* sliced; 1 *undrained* 8-ounce can *lima beans;* and 1 prepared 14-ounce package *deluxe type macaroni-and-cheese mix.* Heat through.

IDEA 5

Stir together one 15-ounce can *chili beans with chili gravy,* 1 prepared 14-ounce package *deluxe type macaroni-and-cheese mix,* and 1 to 2 tablespoons *jalapeño pepper relish.* Heat through.

IDEA 6

Brown ½ pound ground *beef or pork.* Drain off fat. Stir in 1 prepared 14-ounce package *deluxe type macaroni-and-cheese mix* and ⅓ cup *taco sauce.* Heat through.

Four-Cheese Tagliatelle

¼ cup sliced green onion
1 tablespoon margarine *or* butter
⅔ cup light cream
½ cup shredded fontina *or* Gouda cheese (2 ounces)
½ cup crumbled Gorgonzola *or* blue cheese (2 ounces)
½ cup shredded mozzarella cheese (2 ounces)
½ cup grated Parmesan cheese
8 ounces tagliatelle

In a 10-inch skillet cook green onion in hot margarine or butter about 3 minutes or till tender. Reduce heat to low. Stir in cream. Add fontina or Gouda cheese, Gorgonzola or blue cheese, mozzarella cheese, and Parmesan cheese. Cook and stir till cheeses melt. Remove from heat. Set aside.

Meanwhile, cook pasta according to package directions. Immediately drain. Return pasta to the hot kettle or Dutch oven. Add cheese mixture. Toss gently till well mixed. Serve immediately. Makes 4 main-dish servings or 8 side-dish servings.

Microwave: In a 1½-quart nonmetal casserole combine green onion and margarine or butter. Micro-cook, uncovered, on 100% power (high) for 1½ to 2 minutes or till tender. Stir in ½ *cup* light cream, then the fontina or Gouda cheese, Gorgonzola or blue cheese, mozzarella cheese, and Parmesan cheese. Cook, uncovered, for 2 to 2½ minutes more or till cheeses melt, stirring 3 times. Meanwhile, on the *range-top,* cook pasta as above. Immediately drain. Return to the hot kettle or Dutch oven. Add cheese mixture. Toss gently till well mixed.

Fettuccine Alfredo

8 ounces fettuccine
½ cup grated Parmesan cheese
⅓ cup light cream *or* whipping cream, at room temperature
3 tablespoons margarine *or* butter, cut up and at room temperature
Fresh coarsely cracked black pepper

Cook pasta according to package directions.

Immediately drain. Return pasta to the hot kettle or Dutch oven. Add Parmesan cheese, light cream or whipping cream, and margarine or butter. Toss gently till pasta is well coated. Transfer to a warm serving dish. Sprinkle with pepper. Serve immediately. Makes 4 main-dish servings.

Hot Tips on Pasta

Here are three simple tricks for keeping cooked pasta hot:

• Drain the pasta quickly. Don't let it stand in the colander longer than is necessary.

• Return the pasta to the hot cooking pan immediately. The heat of the pan will keep the whole recipe warm.

• Always use a warm serving dish. To warm your serving dish, simply run hot water into it. Let it stand a few minutes to absorb the heat. Then empty the dish and wipe it dry. Add your cooked pasta and serve immediately.

Fettuccine Alfredo

South-of-the-Border Bundles

6 **10-inch flour tortillas**
6 **ounces pasteurized**
    process cheese spread
1 **16-ounce can refried beans**
½ **cup sliced green onions**
1 **4-ounce can green chili**
    peppers, rinsed, seeded,
    and chopped
1 **teaspoon chili powder**
1 **large tomato, cored and**
    chopped
  Taco sauce (optional)
  Sliced green onion

Wrap tortillas tightly in foil. Heat in a 350° oven for 10 minutes. Meanwhile, cut process cheese spread into 6 sticks. In a mixing bowl stir together beans, ½ cup green onions, chili peppers, and chili powder.

Remove *1* tortilla from foil. Spread tortilla with about *½ cup* bean mixture to within 2 inches of the edge. Top with *1 tablespoon* chopped tomato. Place *1* process cheese spread stick in center of tortilla. Fold in 2 sides; roll up. Place on a greased baking sheet. Repeat with remaining tortillas.

Bake in a 350° oven for 15 to 20 minutes or till heated through. To serve, spoon taco sauce atop bundles, if desired. Sprinkle with green onion. Makes 6 servings.

To make the tortillas pliable and easier to work with, wrap them tightly in foil so they don't dry out, then heat them in the oven. Keep the rest of the tortillas covered while you're working with one.

Cut the cheese into sticks measuring 2x1x¾ inches. The sticks need to be approximately this size so they will fit neatly into the bundles.

Working quickly with one heated tortilla at a time, spread some bean mixture on each. Leave a 2-inch border around the edge so the mixture won't spill out of the tortilla.

Spinach Calzones

1 10-ounce package frozen
   chopped spinach
1 3½-ounce package sliced
   pepperoni
2 slightly beaten eggs
1 cup pizza sauce
¼ cup grated Parmesan
   cheese
1 teaspoon dried basil,
   crushed
⅛ teaspoon garlic powder
1 10-ounce package
   refrigerated pizza dough
1 4-ounce package (1 cup)
   shredded mozzarella
   cheese
   Cooking oil
1 tablespoon grated
   Parmesan cheese

Cook spinach according to package directions. Drain, squeezing out excess liquid. Chop pepperoni. Combine spinach, pepperoni, eggs, *¼ cup* of the pizza sauce, the ¼ cup Parmesan cheese, basil, and garlic powder.

Unroll refrigerated dough. Press into a 15x10-inch rectangle. Cut into quarters. Sprinkle mozzarella cheese onto *half* of *each* quarter. Spoon spinach mixture atop. Fold dough over mixture. Seal edges. Place on a greased baking sheet. Brush with oil. Sprinkle with the 1 tablespoon Parmesan. Cut small slits in top of each. Bake in a 450° oven for 10 to 15 minutes or till golden. Heat and pass remaining pizza sauce. Serves 4.

Salmon-Stuffed French Rolls

½ cup chopped broccoli *or*
   cauliflower flowerets
¼ cup shredded carrot
¼ cup chopped cucumber
⅓ cup sandwich spread
½ teaspoon dried dillweed
⅛ teaspoon pepper
1 7¾-ounce can salmon,
   drained, slightly flaked,
   and skin and bones
   removed
3 French-style rolls, split, *or*
   6 slices bread
   Green pepper rings

In a bowl toss together the chopped broccoli or cauliflower flowerets, shredded carrot, and chopped cucumber. Stir in the sandwich spread, dillweed, and pepper. Fold in the flaked salmon. Assemble roll or bread, salmon mixture, and green pepper rings into a sandwich. Makes 3 servings.

Pork-Curry Pockets

⅔ **cup sandwich spread**
¼ **teaspoon curry powder**
1½ **cups finely chopped cooked pork *or* chicken**
⅓ **cup shredded carrot**
¼ **cup coconut**
 2 **tablespoons finely chopped green pepper**
 2 **large pita bread rounds, halved crosswise, *or* 8 slices bread**

In a small bowl stir together the sandwich spread and curry powder. Stir in the finely chopped pork or chicken, carrot, coconut, and green pepper. Mix well. Spoon into pita halves or use bread to assemble into sandwiches. Makes 4 servings.

Cheesy Egg Sandwiches

½ **cup salad dressing *or* mayonnaise**
¼ **teaspoon dry mustard**
⅛ **teaspoon garlic salt**
 3 **hard-cooked eggs, chopped**
 1 **cup shredded cheddar cheese (4 ounces)**
¼ **cup finely chopped celery**
 3 **tablespoons sunflower nuts**
 2 **tablespoons sliced green onion**
 8 **slices sandwich bread**
 8 **tomato slices**
 4 **lettuce leaves (optional)**

In a small bowl stir together the salad dressing or mayonnaise, dry mustard, and garlic salt. Stir in the chopped hard-cooked eggs, shredded cheddar cheese, chopped celery, sunflower nuts, and sliced green onion. Chill thoroughly. For *each* sandwich, spread *½ cup* chilled egg mixture onto *1 slice* of bread. Add *2* tomato slices and *1* lettuce leaf, if desired. Top with *another slice* of bread. Makes 4 sandwiches.

Ham and Fruit Sandwiches

1½ **cups diced fully cooked ham**
 1 **medium apple, cored and chopped (1 cup)**
 1 **8¼-ounce can crushed pineapple, drained**
½ **cup thinly sliced celery**
½ **cup sandwich spread**
 8 **slices raisin bread, toasted and buttered**
 4 **slices Muenster cheese, halved diagonally**
 Apple slices

In a medium mixing bowl stir together the ham, apple, pineapple, celery, and sandwich spread. Spread *each* toast slice with about *⅓ cup* of the ham mixture. Top each with cheese and apple slices. Makes 4 servings.

Tuna Melts

1 **8-ounce jar pasteurized process cheese spread**
¼ **cup salad dressing *or* mayonnaise**
1 **12½-ounce can tuna, drained, and flaked, *or* one 15½-ounce can red salmon, drained, skin and bones removed, and flaked**
1 **8-ounce can sliced water chestnuts, drained and chopped (1 cup)**
2 **tablespoons snipped dried chives**
4 **English muffins, split and toasted**

Combine *½ cup* of the process cheese spread and the salad dressing or mayonnaise. Stir in tuna, water chestnuts, and chives. Spread mixture onto English muffin halves. Place muffins on the unheated rack of a broiler pan. Broil 4 inches from the heat about 3 inches or till heated through. Top each with a dollop of the remaining process cheese spread. Broil for 30 to 60 seconds more or till process cheese spread melts. Serves 4.

Tuna-Egg Saladwiches

1 **9¼-ounce can tuna, drained**
4 **hard-cooked eggs, coarsely chopped**
½ **cup diced celery**
¼ **cup chopped pimiento-stuffed olives**
½ **cup sandwich spread**
1 **tablespoon prepared mustard**
¼ **teaspoon dried tarragon, crushed**
6 **kaiser rolls *or* 12 slices whole wheat bread**
3 **tablespoons margarine *or* butter, softened**
6 **lettuce leaves**

Break tuna into chunks. In a medium mixing bowl combine tuna, hard-cooked eggs, celery, and olives, then set aside.

For dressing, in a small mixing bowl combine sandwich spread, mustard, and tarragon. Add dressing to tuna mixture, then toss. Cover and chill.

To serve, split rolls in half horizontally. Spread cut surfaces with margarine or butter. Spoon tuna mixture onto bottoms of rolls. Top *each* with a lettuce leaf, then a roll top. Serves 6.

Sandwich Wrappers

Bread comes in all shapes, sizes, and flavors. So next time you're preparing a sandwich, match the "wrapper" to the "package." Choose, for example, a dark bread for a robust filling or a light bread for a more delicate filling. Take your pick of light or dark rye, pumpernickel, whole wheat, Russian black, Swedish limpa, or all-American white bread. Or, switch gears and go for croissants, pita bread, bagels, English muffins, or sourdough rolls.

Picnic Pointers

For a picnic that'll come off without a hitch, remember these take-along tips. (1) Make it simple: Choose foods that are easy to prepare, serve, and eat. (2) Be organized: Write list of everything you'll need. Make all the foods ahead and pack them for convenient serving. (3) Keep it safe: To prevent spoilage, serve hot foods hot and cold foods cold. Here are a few more meal-toting hints that will ensure safe, enjoyable, and hassle-free picnics.

● Cut fresh vegetables and fruits into easy-to-eat pieces. Take along a favorite savory dip for the vegetables, and sweet dip for the fruit pieces.

● For easy main dishes, choose already-cooked ham, roast beef, or poultry. Slice the meat or poultry before you go.

● Add muffins or rolls to your cooler or picnic basket. Pack butter, margarine, or other spreads in small airtight containers; carry in the cooler.

● Food can spoil quickly outdoors, especially in the hot sun. To keep food safe, be sure everything that touches picnic food, including your hands, is very clean.

Keep cold foods covered and in ne refrigerator until you leave. hen, pack them in an insulated ontainer with a frozen ice pack.

When you take a hot food, pack at just before you leave, too. Use n insulated container, such as a astic-foam covered casserole, and ck the food as soon as it comes it of the oven or off the range.

Make sure foods that require no eating or chiling are well wrapped. en pack them separately in a picc basket, box or large paper bag.

At the picnic site, don't leave eats, poultry, fish, or dairy prod-ts out after serving. Return left-vers to the cooler or insulated nch box.

● Avoid taking custards, puddings, and other egg-thickened dishes. They can break down and spoil.

● Carry hot and cold beverages — such as coffee, tea lemonade, and fruit juice — in large insulated vac-uum bottles. To keep drinks hot or cold longer, preheat or prechill insulated vacuum bottles before filling.

● Don't forget to pack a tablecloth or blanket paper plates or bowls, plastic eating and serving utensils, plenty of paper napkins, salt and pepper shakers, cups for your bev-erage, and paper towels for spills and cleanup. (To take care of sticky fingers, dampen some of the paper towels and wrap them in small plas-tic bags before you leave home.)

Layered Reuben Salad

2 cups finely shredded
   cabbage
2 cups finely shredded
   lettuce
1 8-ounce bottle Thousand
   Island salad dressing
1 teaspoon caraway seed
2 3-ounce packages sliced
   corn beef, chopped
3 hard-cooked eggs, sliced
1 cup shredded Swiss cheese
   (4 ounces)
4 slices melba toast, coarsely
   crushed

In a mixing bowl combine cabbage, lettuce, *¼ cup* of the Thousand Island salad dressing, and caraway seed. In the bottom of a medium bowl or an 8x8x2-inch dish place *half* of the cabbage mixture. Layer in the following order: *half* of the corned beef, remaining cabbage mixture, remaining corned beef, hard-cooked egg slices, and cheese.

Spread remaining Thousand Island salad dressing evenly over top of salad. Cover tightly with clear plastic wrap. Chill up to 24 hours. Before serving, top with crushed melba toast. Makes 4 main-dish servings.

Ham-And-Artichoke Pasta Salad

6 ounces corkscrew
   macaroni *or* wagon
   wheel macaroni
4 cups ice cubes
4 cups cold water
8 ounces fully cooked ham,
   cubed (about 1½ cups)
1 6½-ounce jar marinated
   artichoke hearts, drained
   and quartered
½ cup buttermilk salad
   dressing
1 2.25-ounce can sliced
   pitted ripe olives, drained
4 lettuce leaves (optional)

Cook pasta according to package directions. Drain well.

Place cooked pasta in a large mixing bowl with ice cubes and the 4 cups cold water. Let stand for 5 minutes. Drain well. Remove any remaining ice cubes.

Meanwhile, in a salad bowl toss together ham, artichoke hearts, salad dressing, and olives. Add macaroni and toss gently to coat. Serve immediately on lettuce leaves, if desired. Makes 4 servings.

Beef and Pasta Salad

4 ounces corkscrew
   macaroni
1 10-ounce package frozen
   cut broccoli
6 ounces thinly sliced
   cooked beef
1 6-ounce jar marinated
   artichoke hearts, drained
2 small tomatoes, cut into
   small wedges
1 cup crumbled feta cheese
   (4 ounces)
½ cup Italian salad dressing

Cook pasta in a large amount of boiling salted water for 9 minutes. Add broccoli. Return to boiling. Cook for 2 to 3 minutes more or till broccoli is crisp-tender. Drain in colander. Rinse with cold water. Drain again.

Meanwhile, cut the beef into julienne strips. Cut up any large artichokes. In a large serving bowl combine beef, artichoke hearts, tomatoes, feta cheese, and pasta mixture.

Add dressing to salad. Toss to coat. Place in the freezer for 10 to 15 minutes to chill, if desired. Makes 4 servings.

Fruity Ham and Pasta Salad

1 11-ounce can mandarin orange sections
1 8¼-ounce can pineapple chunks
1 6¾-ounce can chunk-style ham
1 cup corkscrew macaroni
⅓ cup salad dressing *or* mayonnaise
1 tablespoon honey
2 teaspoons vinegar
¼ teaspoon celery seed
2 cups torn salad greens
1 stalk celery, sliced
2 tablespoons sunflower nuts

Chill unopened cans of oranges, pineapple, and ham in the freezer for 10 minutes. Meanwhile, cook macaroni according to package directions. Drain. Turn macaroni into a bowl of *ice water.* Let stand for 5 minutes. Drain well.

For dressing, in a small bowl stir together salad dressing or mayonnaise, honey, vinegar, and celery seed.

Drain orange sections, pineapple, and ham. Flake ham into chunks.

In a large bowl toss together macaroni, orange sections, pineapple, ham, salad greens, and celery. Pour dressing atop. Toss well to coat. Sprinkle with sunflower nuts. Makes 3 servings.

Honolulu Seafood Salad

1 6 ounces packaged medium noodles
1 medium avocado, halved, seeded, and peeled
   Lemon juice
1 15½-ounce can pineapple chunks, drained
1 7-ounce can crab meat, drained, flaked, and cartilage removed
1 4½-ounce can shrimp, rinsed and drained
½ cup salad dressing *or* mayonnaise
¼ cup dairy sour cream
3 tablespoons sliced green onion
2 tablespoons chili sauce
½ teaspoon Worcestershire sauce
¼ teaspoon dry mustard
   Dash bottled hot pepper sauce
   Lettuce leaves
¼ cup broken pecans

Cook noodles according to package directions. Immediately drain in a colander. Rinse with cold water; drain.

Slice avocado crosswise; brush with lemon juice to prevent darkening. In a mixing bowl combine the cooked noodles, avocado slices, pineapple chunks, crab meat, and shrimp.

For dressing, stir together salad dressing or mayonnaise, sour cream, sliced green onion, chili sauce, Worcestershire sauce, dry mustard, and bottled hot pepper sauce. Spoon dressing over the seafood mixture; toss gently to coat. Cover and chill in the refrigerator for at least 2 hours. Serve on individual lettuce-lined plates. Sprinkle each serving with broken pecans. Makes 4 main-dish servings.

24-Hour Chicken Salad

½ of a medium head iceberg
  lettuce, torn
  (about 4 cups)
1 8-ounce can sliced water
  chestnuts, drained
2 5-ounce cans chunk-style
  chicken, drained and
  broken into large pieces
1 4-ounce package (1 cup)
  shredded cheddar cheese
6 slices bacon, crisp-cooked,
  drained, and crumbled
2 green onions, thinly sliced
  (2 tablespoons)
1 cup salad dressing *or*
  mayonnaise
⅓ cup creamy buttermilk
  salad dressing

Place torn lettuce in a large salad bowl. Top with water chestnuts, then with chicken. If desired, reserve a little cheese and crumbled bacon for garnish; wrap and refrigerate. Sprinkle remaining cheese, remaining bacon, and green onions over chicken.

Stir together salad dressing or mayonnaise and buttermilk salad dressing. Spread mixture atop salad mixture, sealing to the edges of the bowl. Cover and refrigerate for 3 to 24 hours.

At serving time, toss salad. Sprinkle with reserved cheese and bacon, if desired. Serves 4.

Turkey Véronique Salads

1 cup strawberries *or* one
  10½-ounce can mandarin
  orange sections
1½ cups seedless green grapes
2 heads Belgian endive
  Bibb *or* Boston lettuce
  leaves
12 ounces sliced fully cooked
  smoked turkey breast *or*
  plain turkey breast
  Creamy buttermilk salad
  dressing
⅓ cup sliced almonds

Cut strawberries in half or drain mandarin oranges. In a medium mixing bowl combine strawberries or oranges and grapes, then set aside. Separate leaves of Belgian endive.

For the salads, line salad plates with Belgian endive and Bibb or Boston lettuce leaves. Then arrange turkey and fruit on top. Drizzle salad dressing over the salads. Sprinkle with the sliced almonds. Makes 4 servings.

Turkey Véronique Salads

Curried Salmon Salad

1 15½-ounce can red salmon
1 banana, sliced
1 medium apple, chopped
   (1 cup)
   Lemon juice
1½ cups cooked rice
1 small green pepper, cut
   into 1½-inch strips
½ cup salad dressing *or*
   mayonnaise
2 tablespoons milk
1½ to 2 teaspoons curry
   powder
   Lettuce leaves

Remove skin and bones from salmon; break salmon into chunks. Set aside.

For salad, in a large bowl toss banana and chopped apple with a little lemon juice; stir in salmon, cooked rice, and green pepper strips. Cover; chill for several hours.

For dressing, in a small bowl combine salad dressing or mayonnaise, milk, and curry powder. Cover; chill for several hours.

Just before serving, pour dressing over salad; toss lightly to coat. Transfer salmon salad mixture to a lettuce-lined salad bowl. Makes 4 servings.

Cheese-Bean Chowder

3 15-ounce cans pinto *or*
   navy beans, drained
2 cups water
1 medium onion, chopped
1 stalk celery, chopped
2 teaspoons instant beef
   bouillon granules
½ teaspoon dried basil,
   crushed
1 bay leaf
2 cups milk
1 8-ounce jar pasteurized
   process cheese spread
   Snipped parsley

In a Dutch oven combine drained beans, water, onion, celery, bouillon granules, basil, and bay leaf. Bring to boiling. Reduce heat and simmer, covered, for 20 minutes. Discard bay leaf. Mash beans slightly with a fork. Stir in milk and process cheese spread. Cook and stir till process cheese spread melts and soup is heated through. Ladle into soup bowls and garnish with snipped parsley. Makes 5 main-dish servings.

Toppers for Pizzazz

Dress up soups with these quick-as-a-wink ideas:

Use any kind of shredded or grated cheese, purchased bacon pieces, sour cream, yogurt, croutons, nuts, popcorn, crushed crackers, chow mein noodles, fresh herbs and parsley, sliced green onion or avocado, chopped hard-cooked eggs or dill pickles, shredded carrot or zucchini, sliced cucumber or olives, and any kind of sprouts.

Bratwurst-Cheese Soup

¼ **cup margarine *or* butter**
2 **carrots, shredded**
1 **stalk celery, thinly sliced**
¼ **cup all-purpose flour**
⅛ **teaspoon pepper**
4 **cups milk**
8 **ounces smoked bratwurst, sliced**
2 **cups cubed pasteurized process cheese spread (8 ounces)**

In a large saucepan melt the margarine or butter. Add carrots and celery. Cook till tender.

Stir in flour and pepper till blended. Add milk and bratwurst. Cook and stir over medium heat about 8 minutes or till mixture is thickened and bubbly. Cook and stir for 1 minute more.

Add process cheese spread. Cook, stirring constantly, till process cheese spread is melted. Makes 4 servings.

Beer-Cheese Soup

2½ cups water
1 cup beer
¾ cup small shell macaroni
½ teaspoon instant chicken bouillon granules
½ teaspoon minced dried onion
½ teaspoon dried basil, crushed
Several dashes bottled hot pepper sauce
¼ cup cold water
2 tablespoons all-purpose flour
2 cups cubed pasteurized process cheese spread (8 ounces)

In a large saucepan combine 2½ cups water, beer, *uncooked* macaroni, bouillon granules, onion, basil, and hot pepper sauce. Bring to boiling. Reduce heat, then simmer, uncovered, for 10 minutes, stirring occasionally.

Shake ¼ cup water and flour together. Stir flour mixture into hot mixture in the saucepan. Cook and stir till thickened and bubbly. Cook and stir 1 minute more. Stir in process cheese spread. Heat and stir till process cheese spread is melted. Makes 4 servings.

Nacho Potato Soup

2 cups water
1 10-ounce can tomatoes and green chili peppers
1 8-ounce can whole kernel corn
1 4¾-ounce package dry julienne potato mix
Several dashes bottled hot pepper sauce
1½ cups frozen diced cooked chicken
1 cup cubed pasteurized process cheese spread (4 ounces)
½ cup sliced pitted olives
2 cups milk
Tortilla chips

In a 3-quart saucepan combine water, *undrained* tomatoes, *undrained* corn, dry potatoes and seasoning mix from the package, and hot pepper sauce. Bring to boiling. Reduce heat. Cover and simmer about 15 minutes or till potatoes are tender, stirring occasionally.

Stir in chicken, process cheese spread, and olives. Cook and stir till process cheese spread is melted. Stir in milk and heat till mixture is heated through, stirring occasionally. Serve with tortilla chips. Makes 6 servings.

SIDE DISHES

Italian Tortellini Salad

Good Food and Good Food Ideas

TIPS

LEMONY FRUIT SALAD
Combine ½ cup MIRACLE WHIP Salad Dressing or KRAFT Real Mayonnaise with ½ cup lemon flavored yogurt. Serve over or toss with 3 cups assorted fruit combined with ½ cup chopped nuts or coconut. 4 to 6 servings.

BUTTERMILK POTATO SALAD
Combine 4 cups cubed cooked potato, 1 cup celery slices, ½ cup RANCHER'S CHOICE Creamy Dressing, 2 chopped hard-cooked eggs and 2 tablespoons green onion slices; mix lightly. Chill. Add additional dressing before serving, if desired. 4 to 6 servings.

HEAVENLY SEVEN LAYERED SALAD
In 2-quart serving bowl, layer 1-½ qts. shredded lettuce, 2 cups each: chopped tomatoes and sliced mushrooms, 10-oz. pkg. frozen peas, thawed, drained, 4 oz. 100% Natural KRAFT Mild Cheddar Cheese, cubed and 1 cup red onion rings. Spread 2 cups MIRACLE WHIP Salad Dressing over salad, sealing to edge of bowl. Cover; chill several hours or overnight. Garnish with crumbled bacon or shredded cheese, if desired. 8 servings.

QUICK BROCCOLI SIDE DISH
Microwave 10-oz. pkg. frozen chopped broccoli according to label directions; drain. Stir in 4-oz. c mushrooms, drained and oz. jar diced pimento, drained; mix lightly. Micro wave 8-oz. jar CHEEZ WHIZ Pasteurized Proces Cheese Spread accordin to label directions. Serve over broccoli mixture. 3 t servings.

Italian Tortellini Salad   (photo on page 53)

1 7-ounce package cheese-
   filled spinach tortellini
8 ounces provolone cheese
   or mozzarella cheese,
   cubed (2 cups)
1 small tomato, coarsely
   chopped
½ of a small green pepper,
   cut into thin strips
   (¼ cup)
½ cup sliced pitted ripe
   olives, drained
4 green onions, sliced
   (¼ cup)
½ cup Italian salad dressing
¼ cup grated Parmesan
   cheese

Cook tortellini according to package directions.
   Drain tortellini in a colander. Place colander in a large bowl of ice-cold water. Let stand for 5 minutes. Drain well.
   Transfer chilled tortellini to a serving bowl. Add cubed provolone or mozzarella cheese, tomato, pepper strips, olives, and green onions. Pour dressing over tortellini mixture. Toss gently to coat. Add Parmesan cheese and toss lightly. Makes 5 or 6 servings.

Bibb Lettuce with Creamy Italian Dressing

1 cup salad dressing *or*
   mayonnaise
1 8-ounce carton dairy sour
   cream
2 green onions, chopped
2 tablespoons vinegar
2 teaspoons sugar
1 teaspoon Italian seasoning
¾ teaspoon celery salt
¾ teaspoon dry mustard
1 clove garlic, minced
4 small heads Bibb lettuce
   Milk

For dressing, in a small mixing bowl combine salad dressing or mayonnaise, sour cream, onion, vinegar, sugar, Italian seasoning, celery salt, dry mustard, garlic, and ¼ teaspoon *pepper.* Use a wire whisk or rotary beater to mix till smooth. Transfer dressing to a container. Cover and chill till serving time.
   Just before serving, cut each head of lettuce in half lengthwise. Arrange lettuce halves on a serving platter. If desired, garnish platter with cherry tomatoes or radishes and parsley sprigs. If necessary, stir 1 to 2 tablespoons milk into dressing till of desired consistency. Serve dressing with lettuce. Makes 8 servings.

Cucumber and Orange Salad

1 medium cucumber,
   coarsely chopped
   (1¾ cups)
1 16-ounce can mandarin
   orange sections, drained
¼ cup creamy French salad
   dressing *or* creamy
   cucumber salad dressing
¼ teaspoon poppy seed
   Pepper (optional)

In a bowl toss together chopped cucumber, drained orange sections, French or cucumber salad dressing, and poppy seed. Cover and chill in the freezer for 8 minutes. Sprinkle lightly with pepper, if desired. Serves 4.

Pasta Coleslaw

4 ounces packaged tripolini
  (about 1 cup)
4 cups shredded red *or*
  green cabbage
½ cup shredded carrot
2 tablespoons sliced green
  onion
¾ cup salad dressing *or*
  mayonnaise
2 tablespoons vinegar
2 teaspoons sugar
¾ teaspoon dry mustard
½ teaspoon salt
½ teaspoon celery seed

Cook tripolini according to package directions. Immediately drain in a colander. Rinse with cold water; drain.

In a large bowl combine tripolini, cabbage, carrot, and onion. Stir together salad dressing or mayonnaise, vinegar, sugar, dry mustard, salt, and celery seed. Pour over cabbage mixture; toss lightly to coat. Cover and chill for several hours. Makes 8 to 10 side-dish servings.

Tortellini and Cucumber Salad

1 6- *or* 7-ounce package
  frozen tortellini
¼ cup olive oil *or* salad oil
3 tablespoons white *or* rosé
  wine
2 tablespoons lemon juice
1 tablespoon snipped fresh
  basil, tarragon, *or* thyme;
  or 1 teaspoon dried basil,
  tarragon, *or* thyme,
  crushed
1 teaspoon honey
½ teaspoon salt
2 cups torn salad greens
1 small cucumber, halved
  lengthwise and sliced
¾ cup crumbled feta cheese
  (3 ounces)
¼ cup pine nuts *or* slivered
  almonds, toasted

Cook tortellini according to package directions. Drain. Rinse with cold water. Drain well.

For dressing, in a screw-top jar combine oil, wine, lemon juice, herb, honey, and salt. Cover and shake well; pour over tortellini. Cover and chill 2 to 24 hours.

In a large bowl combine pasta, torn greens, cucumber, feta cheese, and pine nuts. Toss to coat. Serve immediately. Serves 5 or 6.

Tangy Herbed Salad Dressing

1 cup salad dressing *or* mayonnaise
2 tablespoons lemon *or* lime juice
1 tablespoon sliced green onion
1 tablespoon milk
1 teaspoon Worcestershire sauce
½ teaspoon dried basil, oregano, thyme, *or* marjoram, crushed
1 clove garlic, minced, *or* ⅛ teaspoon garlic powder
Torn salad greens

In a small bowl stir together salad dressing or mayonnaise; lemon or lime juice; sliced green onion; milk; Worcestershire sauce; dried crushed basil, oregano, thyme, or marjoram; and garlic. Cover and chill at least 1 hour.

Serve atop torn salad greens. Makes about 1¼ cups dressing.

Artichoke and Pasta Salad

1 6-ounce jar marinated artichoke hearts
1 cup cooked corkscrew *or* elbow macaroni
4 ounces cheddar cheese, cut into ½-inch cubes
¼ cup chopped cucumber
1 green onion, sliced
½ cup salad dressing *or* mayonnaise

Drain the artichoke hearts, reserving the marinade.

In a medium bowl combine the drained artichoke hearts, cooked corkscrew or elbow macaroni, cheddar cheese cubes, chopped cucumber, and sliced green onion. Toss to mix well.

For the dressing, in a bowl combine the reserved artichoke marinade and the salad dressing or mayonnaise. Stir to mix well. Pour over the cheese and macaroni mixture; toss gently to coat. Chill till serving time. Makes 2 servings.

Cabbage Plus Slaw

3 cups shredded green cabbage
1 cup shredded red cabbage
1 cup alfalfa sprouts
1 cup shredded carrot
1 cup fresh pea pods *or* frozen pea pods, thawed
½ cup sandwich spread
1 tablespoon milk
¼ teaspoon celery seed
¼ teaspoon salt
½ cup broken walnuts

In a large mixing bowl combine cabbage, alfalfa sprouts, carrot, and pea pods.

For dressing, in a small mixing bowl combine sandwich spread, milk, celery seed, and salt. Pour dressing over cabbage mixture and toss lightly to coat. Cover and chill thoroughly.

Just before serving, gently stir in walnuts. Makes 6 servings.

Italian Vegetable Toss

1½ cups medium shell
    macaroni
1 7½-ounce can artichoke
    hearts
2 cups broccoli flowerets
1 cup cauliflower flowerets
1 cup sliced fresh
    mushrooms
1 cup sliced, pitted ripe
    olives
½ cup sliced green onion
⅔ cup Italian salad dressing
1 medium avocado, seeded,
    peeled, and sliced
1 medium tomato, seeded
    and chopped

Cook macaroni according to package directions. Drain. Rinse with cold water. Drain well. Drain, rinse, and chop artichoke hearts. In a large mixing bowl combine cooked macaroni, chopped artichoke hearts, broccoli, cauliflower, mushrooms, olives, and green onion. Toss with Italian dressing. Cover and chill for several hours. Just before serving, toss vegetable mixture with avocado and tomato. Makes 12 to 16 servings.

Creamy Fruit Dressing

½ cup salad dressing *or*
    mayonnaise
½ cup dairy sour cream
1 tablespoon honey
1 teaspoon poppy seed
½ teaspoon finely shredded
    orange peel
2 to 3 tablespoons orange
    juice *or* milk
Desired fresh fruits, cut up

In a small bowl stir together the salad dressing or mayonnaise, dairy sour cream, honey, poppy seed, and finely shredded orange peel.

Stir in enough orange juice or milk to make the dressing of desired consistency. Spoon over desired cut-up fresh fruit. Makes 1¼ cups dressing.

Chef's Choice Fruit Salad

Romaine leaves
4 cups torn mixed salad
    greens
1 medium apple, cored and
    sliced
¼ cup shredded coconut
1 cup raisins, chopped pitted
    dates, *or* chopped dried,
    pitted prunes
½ cup slivered almonds
½ cup shredded carrot
½ cup salad dressing *or*
    mayonnaise
½ cup dairy sour cream
¼ cup orange marmalade
1 tablespoon milk

Line a large salad bowl with romaine leaves. Place torn mixed greens in center of bowl. Arrange apple slices around the edge of the bowl. Sprinkle with coconut. Arrange raisins, dates, or prunes; almonds; and carrot in a circular design atop lettuce. Cover and chill.

For dressing, combine the salad dressing or mayonnaise, sour cream, marmalade, and milk. Cover and chill.

Just before serving, spoon dressing over salad. Toss to coat. Makes 6 to 8 servings.

Chef's Choice Fruit Salad

Creamy Potato Salad

 6 medium potatoes (2 pounds)
 1 cup thinly sliced celery
 ½ cup finely chopped onion
 ⅓ cup chopped sweet pickle
 1¼ cups salad dressing *or* mayonnaise
 2 teaspoons sugar
 2 teaspoons celery seed
 2 teaspoons vinegar
 2 teaspoons prepared mustard
 2 hard-cooked eggs, coarsely chopped

In a saucepan cook potatoes, covered, in boiling lightly salted water about 25 minutes or till tender. Drain; cool slightly. Using a paring knife, peel potatoes. Cut into bite-size pieces.

In a large bowl combine potatoes, celery, onion, and sweet pickle. For dressing, in a small bowl combine salad dressing or mayonnaise, sugar, celery seed, vinegar, prepared mustard, and 1½ teaspoons *salt*. Pour dressing over potato mixture. Toss to coat. Carefully fold in chopped eggs. Cover and chill 2 to 24 hours. Serves 8.

Cavatelli and Three Cheeses

 8 ounces packaged cavatelli *or* 8 ounces packaged rotelle
 2 tablespoons margarine *or* butter
 2 tablespoons all-purpose flour
 ½ teaspoon salt
 ⅛ teaspoon ground nutmeg
   Dash pepper
 2 cups milk
 1 8-ounce package cream cheese, cut up
 1 cup shredded mozzarella cheese (4 ounces)
 ¼ cup grated Parmesan cheese
 1 medium tomato, sliced (optional)

Cook pasta according to package directions. Rinse with cold water; drain. Set aside.

For cheese sauce in a saucepan melt margarine or butter. Stir in flour, salt, nutmeg, and pepper. Add milk all at once. Cook and stir over medium heat till mixture is thickened and bubbly. Cook and stir 1 minute more. Stir in cream cheese and mozzarella cheese till cheeses are melted.

Gently fold the cooked cavatelli or rotelle into the cheese sauce. Turn mixture into a greased 8x8x2-inch baking dish. Sprinkle with Parmesan cheese. Bake in a 350° oven about 30 minutes or till heated through. Garnish with sliced tomato, if desired. Makes 6 side-dish servings.

Spinach Pesto and Pasta Toss

6 slices bacon
10 ounces spaghetti *or other*
    pasta
1 10-ounce package frozen
    chopped spinach
2 cloves garlic, minced
⅛ teaspoon pepper
½ cup cream-style cottage
    cheese
⅓ cup grated Parmesan
    cheese

In a skillet cook bacon till crisp. Drain, reserving 2 tablespoons drippings. Crumble bacon and set aside. Cook pasta according to package directions.

Meanwhile, in a medium saucepan cook spinach according to package directions. *Do not drain.* Place *undrained* spinach, reserved bacon drippings, garlic, and pepper in a blender container or food processor bowl. Cover and blend or process till smooth. Add *undrained* cottage cheese. Cover and blend or process till smooth.

Arrange pasta on a large serving platter. Pour spinach mixture over pasta. Toss to mix well. Sprinkle with crumbled bacon and Parmesan cheese. Serve immediately. Makes 10 to 12 servings.

Vegetable Garden Primavera

8 ounces linguine *or*
    8 ounces spaghetti
2 medium yellow summer
    squash *or* zucchini, bias-
    sliced into ½-inch
    thick pieces
2 cups broccoli buds
½ pound asparagus, bias-
    sliced into 1-inch-thick
    pieces
2 medium carrots, bias-
    sliced into ¼-inch pieces
1 cup light cream
1 teaspoon dried basil,
    crushed
⅛ teaspoon pepper
2 ounces prosciutto *or* fully
    cooked ham, cut into thin
    strips
½ cup grated Parmesan
    cheese

Cook pasta according to package directions.

Meanwhile, cook the yellow summer squash or zucchini, broccoli, asparagus, and carrots in a small amount of boiling salted water for 5 to 8 minutes or till vegetables are crisp-tender. Drain.

In a saucepan combine light cream, basil, and pepper; bring to a gentle boil. Boil for 8 to 10 minutes or till slightly thickened, stirring occasionally. Stir in prosciutto or ham. Toss together linguine or spaghetti, vegetable mixture, cream mixture, and grated Parmesan cheese. Makes 8 side-dish servings.

Easy Cheesy Potatoes

4 medium potatoes (about 22 ounces total)
½ cup water
1 8-ounce jar process cheese spread with jalapeño peppers

Scrub potatoes thoroughly. Cut potatoes into ¼-inch-thick slices. In a 1½ or 2-quart microwave-safe casserole combine potato slices and water. Micro-cook, covered, on 100% power (high) for 9 to 11 minutes or till potatoes are just tender, stirring after every 3 minutes.

Drain potato slices well. Dollop the process cheese spread onto the potato slices. Cook, uncovered, on high for 45 to 60 seconds or till process cheese spread melts. Gently stir the melted cheese into the potato slices. If thinner consistency is desired, stir in 1-2 tablespoons milk. Makes 4 servings.

Cheesy Scalloped Corn

1 tablespoon margarine *or* butter
8 shredded wheat wafers, crushed (about ½ cup)
1 12-ounce can whole kernel corn with sweet peppers, drained
½ cup cubed pasteurized process cheese spread (2 ounces)
2 tablespoons milk
⅛ teaspoon onion powder

Place margarine or butter in a small microwave-safe bowl or custard cup. Micro-cook, uncovered, on 100% power (high) for 30 to 45 seconds or till melted. Toss with *half* of the crushed wafers. Set aside.

In a 1-quart microwave-safe casserole combine remaining crushed wafers, corn, process cheese spread, milk, and onion powder. Cook, uncovered, on high for 3 to 5 minutes or till process cheese spread melts and mixture is heated through, stirring once. Sprinkle with buttered wafers. Makes 3 or 4 servings.

Quick tip

Easy Measuring
Measuring stick margarine or butter is easy if the wrapper is marked. If your brand doesn't have the markings, just remember that one stick is ½ cup, a half-stick is ¼ cup, and a quarter-stick is 2 tablespoons.

Easy Horseradish Sauce

⅔ cup salad dressing *or*
    mayonnaise
2 tablespoons prepared
    horseradish
2 tablespoons milk
1 teaspoon dry mustard
¼ teaspoon freshly ground
    black pepper

In a small mixing bowl stir together salad dressing or mayonnaise, horseradish, milk, dry mustard, and pepper. Cover and chill thoroughly. Serve with burgers or sandwiches. Makes about ¾ cup.

Broccoli Chowder

1 10-ounce package frozen
    chopped broccoli
1 tablespoon dried minced
    onion
1 10¾-ounce can condensed
    cream of chicken soup
1 cup milk
1 4-ounce package (1 cup)
    shredded cheddar cheese
⅛ teaspoon ground red
    pepper
¼ cup peanuts, chopped
    (optional)

In a medium saucepan bring ½ cup *water* to boiling. Add broccoli and onion. Cover and simmer about 5 minutes or till broccoli is crisp-tender. *Do not* drain. Stir in condensed soup, milk, cheese, and pepper. Cook and stir about 4 minutes or till heated through. Pass peanuts to sprinkle atop soup, if desired. Makes 4 or 5 servings.

Quick tip

Speedy Cheese Sauce
Turn an ordinary vegetable into the highlight of the meal by adding a quick cheese sauce.

Simply stir some process cheese spread or soft-style cream cheese into well-drained, cooked vegetables. Cook and stir till the cheese melts and is heated through. Vary the flavor by using different cheese spreads or by adding a few dashes of bottled hot pepper sauce.

Mayo-Parmesan Bread

½ cup grated Parmesan
  cheese
½ cup salad dressing *or*
  mayonnaise
2 tablespoons snipped chives
  or parsley (optional)
8 *to* 10 slices French *or*
  Italian bread, cut ½ inch
  thick

In a small mixing bowl combine Parmesan cheese and salad dressing or mayonnaise. Stir in snipped chives or parsley, if desired. Set aside.

Place French or Italian bread slices on the rack of an unheated broiler pan. Broil 3 to 4 inches from heat about 1 minute or till toasted.

Turn bread over. Spread some of the salad dressing or mayonnaise mixture on the untoasted side of each slice of bread. Broil, salad dressing side up, 3 to 4 inches from heat for 2 to 3 minutes or till light brown. Makes 4 or 5 servings.

DESSERTS

Mocha-Rum Cheesecake

KRAFT TIPS

FUDGEMALLOW CANDY

Microwave 12-oz. pkg. semi-sweet chocolate pieces and 1 cup chunk style peanut butter in 2-quart bowl on Medium (50%) 2 to 3 minutes or until chocolate is melted, stirring after each minute. Fold in 4 cups KRAFT Miniature Marshmallows. Spread into greased 9-inch square pan; chill until firm. Cut into squares. Approximately 2 dozen.

CHOCOLATE CREAM MOUSSE

Whip 1 cup whipping cream until stiff peaks form; set aside. Combine 3-oz. pkg. PHILADELPHIA BRAND Cream Cheese, softened, ½ cup semi-sweet chocolate pieces, melted and 1 teaspoon vanilla, mixing at medium speed on electric mixer until well blended. Blend in 7-oz. jar KRAFT Marshmallow Creme. Fold in whipped cream. Pour into 1-quart serving bowl; chill several hours. 6 to 8 servings.

CARAMEL CORN

Pop enough popcorn to yield 2½ quarts; set aside. Microwave 28 KRAFT Caramels and 2 tablespoons water in medium bowl on High, 1½ minutes; stir. Continue microwaving 30 seconds to 1 minute, until sauce is smooth, stirring every 30 seconds. Pour immediately over popped corn; toss until well coated. Spread onto greased cookie sheet to form single layer. Bake at 250°, 20 to 25 minutes; break apart. 2½ quarts.

ROCKY ROAD CAKE

Prepare 2-layer chocolate cake mix as directed on package for 13 x 9-inch cake. Sprinkle 3 cups KRAFT Miniature Marshmallows over hot cake. Continue baking at 350°, 2 to 3 minutes or until marshmallows are softened. Sprinkle with ½ cup chopped nuts. Melt ½ cup semi-sweet chocolate pieces with two tablespoons milk over low heat, stirring until smooth. Drizzle over marshmallows and nuts. Cool. 12 servings.

Key Lime-Chocolate Pie

16 chocolate sandwich
   cookies, crushed (½ cup)
½ cup coconut
2 tablespoons margarine *or*
   butter, melted
3 egg yolks
1 14-ounce can (1¼ cups)
   sweetened condensed
   milk
2 envelopes (2 ounces)
   premelted unsweetened
   chocolate product
⅓ cup lime juice
3 egg whites
1 7-ounce jar marshmallow
   creme

Combine crushed cookies, coconut, and margarine or butter. Spread evenly in a 9-inch pie plate. Press onto bottom and up sides to form a firm, even crust. Bake in a 375° oven about 8 minutes or till done. Cool.

   Meanwhile, beat egg yolks about 4 minutes or till thick and lemon colored. Add sweetened condensed milk, chocolate, and lime juice. Beat till combined. Pour into prepared crust.

   Wash beaters. Beat egg whites till soft peaks form. Gradually add marshmallow creme, beating till stiff peaks form. Spread over filling, sealing to edges of crust. Bake in a 350° oven for 12 to 15 minutes or till meringue is golden. Cool slightly. Chill. Makes 8 servings.

Mocha-Rum Cheesecake   (photo on page 65)

1½ cups finely crushed crisp
   oatmeal cookies (12 to
   14 cookies)
¼ cup margarine *or* butter,
   melted
¼ cup rum
1 tablespoon instant coffee
   crystals
3 8-ounce packages cream
   cheese, softened
1 cup sugar
4 squares (4 ounces)
   semisweet chocolate,
   melted and cooled
2 tablespoons all-purpose
   flour
1 teaspoon vanilla
3 eggs
   Whipped cream (optional)
   Chocolate curls (optional)
   Fresh *or* frozen-and-
   thawed raspberries
   (optional)
   Fresh mint leaves
   (optional)

In a mixing bowl toss together crushed cookies and margarine or butter till well combined. Press onto the bottom and 1½ inches up the sides of a 9-inch springform pan.

   Stir together rum and coffee crystals. In a large mixer bowl beat cream cheese, sugar, chocolate, flour, and vanilla just till combined. Add eggs all at once. Beat just till combined. *Do not overbeat.* Stir in rum mixture. Pour mixture into crumb crust.

   Bake in a 350° oven for 50 to 60 minutes or till center appears to be set; cool for 10 minutes. With a knife or small metal spatula loosen sides of cheesecake from pan; remove sides of pan. Let cheesecake stand at room temperature about 2 hours or till cool. Chill till serving time.

   Garnish with whipped cream, chocolate curls, raspberries, and mint leaves, if desired. Makes 12 servings.

Individual Praline Cheesecakes

1 8-ounce package cream cheese, softened
½ cup packed brown sugar
1 teaspoon vanilla
2 eggs
1½ cups dairy sour cream
12 graham cracker tart shells
36 pecan halves

In a smaller mixer bowl beat cream cheese till smooth. Add sugar and vanilla; beat till well combined. Add eggs all at once. Beat just till combined. *Do not overbeat.* Stir in sour cream.

Pour mixture into tart shells. Bake in a 350° oven for 15 to 18 minutes or till center appears set; cool. Place 3 pecan halves on top of each cheesecake in a spokelike fashion. Chill till serving time. Makes 12 servings.

Pineapple-Orange Squares

¾ cup all-purpose flour
½ cup coconut
⅓ cup margarine *or* butter, melted
2 tablespoons brown sugar
1 quart vanilla ice cream
1 8-ounce package cream cheese, softened
½ of a 6-ounce can (⅓ cup) frozen orange juice concentrate, thawed
1 8¼-ounce can crushed pineapple drained
   Pineapple slices (optional)

Stir together flour, coconut, margarine or butter, and brown sugar. Spread evenly in an 8x8x2-inch baking pan. Press onto bottom of pan to form a firm, even crust. Bake in a 325° oven about 20 minutes or till golden. Cool.

Meanwhile, stir ice cream to soften. Beat cream cheese and orange juice concentrate till fluffy. Add ice cream by spoonfuls, beating till smooth after each addition. Stir in crushed pineapple. Spoon into prepared crust. Freeze 8 hours or overnight. Let stand 10 minutes before serving. Garish with pineapple slices, if desired. Serves 8 or 9.

Peanut Butter and Cream Cheese Pie

1 8-ounce package cream cheese, cut up
½ cup peanut butter
1 cup sifted powdered sugar
2 tablespoons milk
1 4-ounce container frozen whipped dessert topping, thawed
1 chocolate-flavored crumb pie shell, graham cracker crumb pie shell, *or* butter-flavored crumb pie shell
   Coarsely chopped peanuts (optional)

In a large mixer bowl combine cream cheese and peanut butter; beat with an electric mixer till combined. Add powdered sugar and milk; beat till combined. Fold in whipped topping. Spoon into the pie shell. Sprinkle with peanuts, if desired. Cover and chill in the freezer for 15 minutes. Makes 8 servings.

Cottage Cheese Cheesecake

1½ cups finely crushed
    graham crackers
⅓ cup margarine *or* butter,
    melted
¼ cup sugar
1 cup cream-style cottage
    cheese
2 8-ounce packages cream
    cheese, softened
¾ cup sugar
2 tablespoons all-purpose
    flour
2 teaspoons vanilla
3 eggs
¼ cup light cream *or* milk
1 8-ounce carton dairy sour
    cream
1 cup sliced fresh fruit

For crust, in a mixing bowl stir together crushed graham crackers, margarine or butter, and ¼ cup sugar. Press mixture evenly over the bottom and 1¾ inches up sides of a 9-inch springform pan. Place the pan in a shallow baking pan.

For filling, in a large mixer bowl beat *undrained* cottage cheese till almost smooth. Beat in cream cheese, ¾ cup sugar, flour, and vanilla. Add eggs all at once, then beat with an electric mixer on low speed just till mixed. *Do not overbeat.* Stir in cream or milk. Pour filling into the crumb-lined pan.

Bake in a 350° oven for 50 to 60 minutes or till done. Cool on a wire rack for 5 to 10 minutes. Loosen sides of cheesecake. Spread sour cream over top. Cool 30 minutes more. Remove sides of pan. Cover and chill 4 to 24 hours. To serve, arrange fruit atop cheesecake. Serves 12 to 14.

Cream Cheese Tart

½ of a 15-ounce package (1
    crust) folded refrigerated
    unbaked piecrusts
¼ cup coconut
1 8-ounce container
    soft-style cream cheese
    with pineapple
1 11-ounce can pineapple
    tidbits and mandarin
    orange sections, well
    drained

Let piecrust stand at room temperature for 5 minutes. Unfold the piecrust onto a baking sheet. Fold in the edges of the piecrust to make a 9-inch circle. Flute edges of piecrust to form a ½-inch-high rim. Prick bottom of the crust. Bake in a 450° oven for 8 to 10 minutes or till golden.

If desired, place coconut in a shallow baking pan and bake in a 450° oven for 2 to 3 minutes or till golden, stirring often.

Spread cream cheese evenly over the baked crust. Arrange pineapple and oranges over crust and sprinkle with coconut. Cut into wedges to serve. Cover any remaining tart and store in the refrigerator. Serves 6 to 8.

Quick Crème de Menthe Pie

Fix'n **Freeze**

25 **chocolate wafers, crushed**
   (1⅓ cups)
 6 **tablespoons margarine *or***
   butter, melted
 1 **7-ounce jar marshmallow**
   creme
¼ **cup green crème de**
   menthe
½ **cup finely chopped layered**
   chocolate-mint candies
   (16 rectangles)
 2 **cups whipping cream**

In a mixing bowl toss together crushed wafers and margarine or butter till well combined. Press crumb mixture firmly onto bottom and up the sides of a 9-inch pie plate; set aside. In a large mixer bowl beat marshmallow creme and crème de menthe with an electric mixer till smooth. Fold in candy. In a small mixer bowl beat whipping cream till soft peaks form (tips curl). Fold into marshmallow mixture. Spoon into the crumb crust. Freeze, uncovered, for 1 to 2 hours or till firm. Remove from freezer. Seal, label, and freeze.

To serve, unwrap frozen pie. Set the pie plate on a warm, damp towel. Makes 8 servings.

Some Freezer Tips

To make the most efficient use of your freezer, keep these points in mind:

• Set your freezer temperature at 0° F or below to maintain the best food color, flavor, and texture. A freezer thermometer will help you check on the temperature in your freezer.

• When you add a casserole to the freezer, separate it from the other packages until it's solidly frozen. This allows the cold air to circulate around the casserole.

• Let foods freeze as quickly as possible by limiting how much food you add to the freezer at one time. Freeze only two to three pounds of food per cubic foot of total storage space within a 24-hour period.

• Freeze casseroles up to three months. Label and date each casserole when you freeze it.

Then you can quickly identify the package and know when to use it.

• To keep your baking dishes and casseroles free for cooking, wrap your make-ahead recipes this way: Cut a length of heavy-duty foil three times the width or diameter of the dish. Line the casserole or dish with the foil. Add the food and cool. Bring the longer sides of the foil together over the food. Fold down the foil, pressing the air out, until the foil is next to the food. Fold down the shorter sides of the foil. Freeze until firm. Then lift the foil-wrapped food from the dish. Label and store in the freezer. When you're ready to reheat, remove the foil and return the frozen food to the original dish. You'll get an exact fit every time.

Polka-Dot Dessert

1 4-serving-size package *instant* chocolate pudding mix
2 cups milk
1 pint peppermint *or* mint chocolate chip ice cream, softened
1 cup flavored tiny marshmallows

Place pudding mix in a large mixer bowl. Add milk. Beat with an electric mixer on medium speed for 2 minutes.

Fold softened ice cream into pudding mixture. Turn into an 8x8x2-inch pan. Sprinkle marshmallows on top. Freeze. Let stand for 15 minutes before serving. Makes 9 servings.

Chewy Granola Goodies

1 10-ounce package regular marshmallows
¼ cup margarine *or* butter
4 cups granola with raisins
1½ cups crisp rice cereal
½ cup sunflower nuts

Line a 13x9x2-inch pan with foil. Butter foil. Set aside.

In a large saucepan combine the marshmallows and margarine or butter. Cook and stir mixture till the marshmallows are melted.

Stir in granola with raisins, crisp rice cereal, and sunflower nuts.

Press mixture into the prepared pan. Cool. Remove foil lining with uncut bars from pan. Cut into bars. Makes 24.

Fruited Rum Balls

1½ cups crushed graham
      crackers (about 20
      graham cracker squares)
  1 6-ounce package mixed
      dried fruit bits (1½ cups)
  1 cup chopped pecans
  1 7-ounce jar marshmallow
      creme
 ⅓ cup rum
  1 teaspoon finely shredded
      lemon peel
 ¼ teaspoon ground
      cinnamon
 ¼ teaspoon ground nutmeg
  1 cup coconut

In a bowl stir together graham crackers, dried fruit bits, and pecans. Set aside. In a 1-quart saucepan combine marshmallow creme, rum, lemon peel, cinnamon, and nutmeg. Cook and stir over low heat till marshmallow creme is melted and mixture is well combined. Pour over dried fruit mixture, stirring till well combined. Cover and chill for 2 or 3 hours or till firm.

Shape chilled fruit mixture into 1-inch balls, then roll in coconut. Wrap fruit balls individually in plastic wrap. Store in an airtight container. (Balls can be frozen for up to 6 months.) Makes about 42.

Caramel Pecan Brownies

 ⅔ cup vanilla caramels
      (12 caramels)
 ⅓ cup margarine *or* butter
  2 tablespoons milk
 ¾ cup sugar
  2 eggs
 ½ teaspoon vanilla
 ¾ cup all-purpose flour
 ½ teaspoon baking powder
 ¼ teaspoon salt
 ½ cup chopped pecans

In a 2-quart saucepan combine the caramels, margarine or butter, and milk. Heat and stir over low heat just till caramels are melted. Remove the saucepan from the heat. Stir in the sugar. Add the eggs and vanilla; stir till well blended. Set aside.

In a mixing bowl combine flour, baking powder, and salt. Add to saucepan mixture, stirring till blended. Stir in pecans. Turn into a greased 9x9x2-inch baking pan.

Bake in a 350° oven for 20 to 25 minutes or till a wooden toothpick inserted in the center comes out clean. Cool in pan on a wire rack; cut into bars. Makes about 20 bars.

Cinnamon-Marshmallow Squares

1 **10-ounce package marshmallows**
¼ **cup margarine *or* butter**
4 **cups crisp rice cereal**
2 **cups cornflakes, slightly crushed**
½ **cup red cinnamon candies *or* raisins**

Line a 9x9x2-inch baking pan with foil, extending foil over the edges of the pan. Butter the foil. Set pan aside.

In a large saucepan melt marshmallows and margarine or butter over low heat, stirring constantly. Remove pan from heat. Add rice cereal, cornflakes, and cinnamon candies or raisins, stirring till combined. Press mixture evenly into prepared pan. Let stand till firm. Use the foil to lift mixture out of pan. Peel off the foil. Cut into squares. Makes 18.

Rocky-Road Brownie Pizza

Nonstick spray coating *or* shortening
1 **roll refrigerated brownie dough**
½ **of a 7-ounce jar marshmallow creme**
⅓ **cup chopped nuts**
⅓ **cup miniature semisweet chocolate pieces**

Preheat the oven to 350°. Spray a 12-inch pizza pan with nonstick spray coating or grease with shortening. Spread dough over bottom of pan.

Bake in the 350° oven for 25 to 30 minutes or till done. Cool in pan on a wire rack for 10 minutes. Transfer to a serving plate.

Immediately dollop with marshmallow creme. Let stand for 1 minute to soften, then spread evenly. Sprinkle with chopped nuts and chocolate pieces. Cut into wedges to serve. Serve warm or cool. Makes 16 to 20 servings.

Pound Cake Fix-Up

Slice a frozen loaf *pound cake*, thawed, horizontally in half. Spread *soft-style cream cheese* on bottom layer, then top with *preserves*. Replace top cake layer. Top with *soft-style cream cheese* and melted *preserves*.

Chewy Caramel Popcorn Balls

½ **of a 14-ounce package
  vanilla caramels**
1 **tablespoon water**
2 **teaspoons margarine *or*
  butter**
7 **cups popped popcorn***
  Margarine *or* butter

Combine caramels, water, and 2 teaspoons margarine or butter into a 4-cup liquid measuring cup. Micro-cook, uncovered, on 100% power (high) for 1½ minutes. Use a rubber scraper to stir till smooth. If caramels aren't soft enough to stir smooth, micro-cook for 30 to 60 seconds more.

Put the popcorn into a large microwave-safe mixing bowl. Pour the melted caramel mixture over the popcorn. Use 2 rubber scrapers to toss gently till popcorn is coated with caramel.

Rub a little margarine or butter onto your hands. Shape the popcorn into 8 medium-size balls, putting balls onto waxed paper-lined baking sheet after shaping. If the caramel corn gets too cool to stick together while shaping, micro-cook, uncovered, on high for 30 seconds or till caramel mixture is sticky again. Makes 8 popcorn balls.

*Note: Substitute 6 cups popped popcorn **and** 1 cup granola or other ready-to-eat cereal for the 7 cups popped popcorn, if desired.

Fluttering Butterflies

  Margarine *or* butter
¼ **cup finely chopped nuts**
48 **small twisted pretzels**
½ **of a 14-ounce package
  vanilla caramels**
1 **tablespoon milk**
1 **tablespoon margarine
  or butter**
48 **inches red *or* black
  shoestring licorice, cut
  into 1-inch pieces**
½ **of a 6-ounce package
  (½ cup) semisweet
  chocolate pieces**

Grease a large baking sheet with margarine or butter. For the base of *each* butterfly, sprinkle about ½ *teaspoons* of the finely chopped nuts in a small circle on the greased baking sheet. Space nut circles 2 inches apart. Make *each* butterfly's wings by arranging *2* pretzels together atop a nut circle. Set aside.

Combine caramels, milk, and the 1 tablespoon margarine or butter in a 4-cup liquid measuring. Micro-cook, uncovered, on 100% power (high) for 1½ minutes. Use a rubber scraper to stir till smooth. If caramels aren't soft enough to stir smooth, micro-cook for 30 to 60 seconds more. Spoon *1 teaspoon* caramel mixture onto *each* set of two pretzels. (Push caramel off teaspoon with a small spoon.)

For antennae, press *2* pieces of licorice into *each* butterfly. Chill, uncovered, for 30 minutes or till firm. Put chocolate pieces into a 2-cup liquid measuring cup. Micro-cook, uncovered, on high for 1 to 1½ minutes or till melted. Spoon about ½ *teaspoon* chocolate onto *each* butterfly. Chill about 15 minutes or till chocolate is firm. Store in a single layer in a tightly covered container. Makes 24 butterflies.

Quick Caramel Topping

25 vanilla caramels
2 tablespoons water

In a 4-cup measure cook caramels and water, uncovered, on 100% power (high) for 2 to 3 minutes or till soft enough to stir smooth, stirring once. Top ice cream. Makes ¾ cup (6 servings).

Peanut Butter Fudge

Margarine *or* butter
4 cups sugar
1⅓ cups milk
1 12-ounce package semisweet chocolate pieces
1 cup creamy peanut butter
¼ cup margarine *or* butter
1 7-ounce jar marshmallow creme
1 cup chopped peanuts
2 teaspoons vanilla

Butter a 13x9x2-inch baking pan and the sides of a heavy 3-quart saucepan; set baking pan aside. In saucepan combine sugar and milk. Cook and stir over medium heat till sugar dissolves and mixture comes to boiling. Cook without stirring to soft ball stage (234°). Remove from heat. Stir in chocolate pieces, peanut butter, and margarine or butter till well combined. Stir in marshmallow creme, peanuts, and vanilla till well combined. Pour into buttered 13x9x2-inch baking pan. Score in squares while warm; cut when firm. Store in refrigerator. Makes about 3½ pounds.

Marshmallow-Chocolate Sauce

1 cup tiny marshmallows
1 6-ounce package (1 cup) semisweet chocolate *or* butterscotch-flavored pieces
¼ cup milk

In a 4-cup measure combine marshmallows, chocolate or butterscotch pieces, and milk. Cook, uncovered, on 100% power (high) for 1 to 2 minutes or till mixture is hot and marshmallows and pieces are soft enough to stir smooth, stirring once during cooking. Serve warm over ice cream or cake slices. Makes 1 cup (8 servings).

Caramel Cereal Pops

 1 14-ounce package vanilla
       caramels
 ¼ cup milk
 4 cups crisp rice cereal
 1 cup salted peanuts
 16 wooden sticks

In a heavy 3-quart saucepan combine caramels and milk. Cook and stir over low heat till caramels are melted and smooth. Stir in the cereal and peanuts till well coated with caramel mixture. Press the cereal mixture into a greased 8x8x2-inch baking pan. Let stand about 1 hour or till firm. Cut into 2-inch squares. Insert a wooden stick into one end of each square. Makes 16 pops.

Rocky Road Drops

 1 6-ounce package (1 cup)
       semisweet chocolate
       pieces
 6 ounces chocolate- *or*
       vanilla-flavored
       confectioners' coating,
       cut up
 1½ cups peanut butter cereal
 1 cup tiny marshmallows
 ¾ cup peanuts

Line a cookie sheet with waxed paper. Set aside. In a medium heavy saucepan melt chocolate pieces and confectioners' coating over low heat, stirring often. Remove pan from heat.

In a medium mixing bowl stir together cereal, marshmallows, and peanuts. Add cereal mixture to melted chocolate, stirring till combined. Drop by rounded teaspoons on the prepared cookie sheet. Chill about 1 hour or till firm. Store tightly covered in the refrigerator. Makes about 36.

Caramel Apple People

 8 wooden sticks
 8 medium apples
 1 14-ounce package vanilla
       caramels
 2 tablespoons water
 ½ cup sunflower nuts,
       miniature semisweet
       chocolate pieces, *or*
       Grape Nuts cereal
    Assorted candies and nuts*

Push a wooden stick into the stem end of each apple; set aside. In a 4-cup liquid measuring cup combine caramels and water. Micro-cook, uncovered, on 100% power (high) for 2 minutes; stir with a rubber scraper. Micro-cook on high for 30 seconds to 1 minute and 30 seconds more or till melted. Stir till smooth.

Put sunflower nuts, chocolate pieces, or cereal onto waxed paper; set aside. Dip each apple into the hot caramel, using a spoon to spread the mixture evenly over apple. Hold the apple over the caramel to allow the excess to drip off into the measuring cup. Dip the bottom of apple into the sunflower nuts, chocolate pieces, or cereal. To hold the apple upright, turn 8 plastic foam cups upside down and push sticks through bottoms. (*Or*, place apples upside down on waxed paper.)

While the caramel coating is still warm, use candies and nuts to decorate the apples, making them look like people. Makes 8 servings.

Note: Use shoestring licorice, fruit-flavored circle candies, candy corn, candy-coated milk chocolate pieces, gumdrop halves, cashews, and sliced almonds.

Caramel Apple People